IT4IT™ FOR MANAGING

A MANAGEME

The Open Group Publications available from Van Haren Publishing

The TOGAF Series:
TOGAF® Version 9.1
TOGAF® Version 9.1 – A Pocket Guide
TOGAF® 9 Foundation Study Guide, 3rd Edition
TOGAF® 9 Certified Study Guide, 3rd Edition

The Open Group Series:
The IT4IT™ Reference Architecture, Version 2.0
IT4IT™ for Managing the Business of IT – A Management Guide
The IT4IT™ Reference Architecture, Version 2.0 – A Pocket Guide
Cloud Computing for Business – The Open Group Guide
ArchiMate® 2.1 – A Pocket Guide
ArchiMate® 2.1 Specification
ArchiMate® 2 Certification – Study Guide

The Open Group Security Series:
Open Information Security Management Maturity Model (O-ISM3)
Open Enterprise Security Architecture (O-ESA)
Risk Management – The Open Group Guide
The Open FAIR™ Body of Knowledge – A Pocket Guide

All titles are available to purchase from:
www.opengroup.org
www.vanharen.net
and also many international and online distributors.

IT4IT™ for Managing the Business of IT

A Management Guide

Rob Akershoek et al.

Title:	IT4IT™ for Managing the Business of IT – A Management Guide
Series:	The Open Group Series
A Publication of:	The Open Group
Author:	Rob Akershoek et al.
Publisher:	Van Haren Publishing, Zaltbommel, www.vanharen.net
ISBN Hardcopy:	978 94 018 0031 0
ISBN eBook:	978 94 018 0592 6
ISBN ePub:	978 94 018 0593 3
Edition:	First edition, first impression, January 2016
Layout and Cover Design:	CO2 Premedia, Amersfoort – NL

IT4IT™ for Managing the Business of IT – A Management Guide
Document Number: G160
Published by The Open Group, January 2016.
Comments relating to the material contained in this document may be submitted to:
The Open Group
Apex Plaza
Reading
Berkshire, RG1 1AX
United Kingdom
or by electronic mail to: ogspecs@opengroup.org

Contents

Preface

The Open Group

The Open Group is a global consortium that enables the achievement of business objectives through IT standards. With more than 500 member organizations, The Open Group has a diverse membership that spans all sectors of the IT community – customers, systems and solutions suppliers, tool vendors, integrators, and consultants, as well as academics and researchers – to:

- Capture, understand, and address current and emerging requirements, and establish policies and share best practices
- Facilitate interoperability, develop consensus, and evolve and integrate specifications and open source technologies
- Offer a comprehensive set of services to enhance the operational efficiency of consortia
- Operate the industry's premier certification service

Further information on The Open Group is available at www.opengroup.org.

The Open Group publishes a wide range of technical documentation, most of which is focused on development of Open Group Standards and Guides, but which also includes white papers, technical studies, certification and testing documentation, and business titles. Full details and a catalog are available at www.opengroup.org/bookstore.

Readers should note that updates – in the form of Corrigenda – may apply to any publication. This information is published at www.opengroup.org/corrigenda.

About the IT4IT™ Forum

The Open Group IT4IT Forum was established in October 2014. It develops and maintains the IT4IT Reference Architecture. The mission of The Open Group IT4IT Forum is to create and drive the adoption of the IT4IT standard that provides a vendor-neutral Reference Architecture for managing the business of IT, enabling insight for agile improvement with increased focus on business outcomes.

For more information on The Open Group IT4IT Forum, visit www.opengroup.org/IT4IT.

About the IT4IT™ Standard

- IT4IT, an Open Group standard, provides a vendor-neutral, technology-agnostic, and industry-agnostic reference architecture for managing the business of IT, enabling insight for continuous improvement.
- IT4IT provides the capabilities for managing the business of IT that will enable IT execution across the entire value chain in a better, faster, cheaper way with less risk.
- IT4IT is industry-independent to solve the same problems for everyone.
- IT4IT is designed for existing landscapes and accommodates new IT paradigms such as cloud-brokering, DevOps, Bimodal IT, Agile, and Lean IT.
- IT4IT complements existing process frameworks and methodologies (e.g., ITIL®, COBIT®, and the TOGAF® standard) by taking a data-focused and solution oriented implementation model perspective, essentially specifying what information is needed and how IT activities can be automated across the entire value chain.

This Document

This document is the IT4IT Management Guide. It provides guidance on how the IT4IT Reference Architecture can be used within an IT organization to manage the business of IT. It is designed to provide a guide to business managers, CIOs, IT executives, IT professionals, and all individuals involved or interested in how to transition an IT organization to become a Lean and Agile IT service provider.

After reading this document you should be able to:
- Understand why the IT4IT approach is needed to improve the performance of the IT function; and support the business to leverage new IT in the digital age
- Understand the vision, scope, and content of the IT4IT Reference Architecture (from a high-level perspective)
- Understand the benefits of using the IT4IT Reference Architecture within the IT function
- Initiate the first steps to implement the IT4IT standard in your own IT organization

After many years of improving IT management capabilities, applying many best practices (and standards), configuring countless IT management tools, and defining dozens of IT processes, most IT organizations have to admit they are still not in control. They now realize that a different approach is needed because they lost sight of the bigger picture as a result of organizing in silos, focusing on individual processes, teams, and tools. This hinders the IT function to establish end-to-end workflows, which is vitally needed to enhance the value of IT for the business. The IT4IT Reference Architecture and value chain-based IT operating model are designed to provide a holistic and integrated foundation for IT management that offers this fundamentally different approach to managing the business of IT.

The IT Value Chain and IT4IT Reference Architecture represent the IT service lifecycle in a new and powerful way. They provide the missing link between industry standard best practice guides and the technology framework and tools that power the service management ecosystem. They provide a new foundation of how to organize and run the business of IT. Together, they deliver a welcome blueprint for the CIO to accelerate IT's transition in becoming a service broker and service integrator focusing on delivering value to the business. They also address management challenges brought about by new technologies or trends such as mobility, cloud, big data, security, Internet of Things (IoT), containers, Software-Defined Networking (SDN), and Bring Your Own Device (BYOD).

Organizing the IT operating model based on the IT4IT Reference Architecture allows organizations to:
- Focus on the true role of IT: to deliver added-value services that makes the company more competitive and innovative
- Become more responsive to deliver changes and act upon a continuously changing technology and business landscape (becoming a Lean and Agile IT function)
- Support the multi-sourced service economy; enable new experiences in driving the self-sourcing of services that power innovation
- Improve the overall performance and efficiency of the IT function and its capabilities to deliver exceeding expectations
- Create an efficient and streamlined IT service organization by automating IT activities from an end-to-end value stream perspective
- Attract and retain the vital IT skills and competences required to manage the new IT ecosystem

- Control risks associated with IT to ensure secure and reliable operations for the business

Adoption of the IT4IT Reference Architecture enables an IT organization to optimize the IT management activities throughout the IT service lifecycle by creating a more mature and professional IT function. This is realized by implementing a standard-based holistic IT management capability, integrating tools from different vendors, supporting (and automating) end-to-end workflows, and providing standard interfaces to collaborate with external service providers while leveraging established best practices.

The audience for this Management Guide is:
- CIOs and other IT executive managers who would like to transform their IT organization to support end-to-end value streams
- Senior leaders and executives in the business and IT responsible for how IT is organized, managed, and improved
- Enterprise Architects involved in the implementation of IT management solutions within the IT organization
- IT professionals and consultants involved in the transition of their organizations to a new streamlined IT factory

Prior knowledge of IT Service Management (ITSM) and related frameworks such as ITIL is advantageous but not required.

This Management Guide is structured as follows:
- Chapter 1 provides an executive summary of this Management Guide.
- Chapter 2 provides an introduction to the IT4IT standard (and IT management in general), the challenges, and the key drivers for changing the way IT is managed today. It also describes how the IT4IT standard fits into the overall landscape of best practices and standards such as ITIL.
- Chapter 3 introduces the IT4IT value streams and provides an overview of the IT4IT Reference Architecture.
- Chapter 4 explains why the IT4IT Reference Architecture is needed and what value it brings to the business and the IT function itself.
- Chapter 5 describes how the IT4IT Reference Architecture is best used and how to implement the standard within your own IT organization.

The appendix contains two case studies of organizations that have applied the IT4IT Reference Architecture. The appendix also contains the mapping of the IT4IT standard and other relevant best practices, frameworks, and standards.

Conventions Used in this Management Guide

The following conventions are used throughout this Management Guide in order to help identify important information and avoid confusion over the intended meaning.

- Ellipsis (…)
  Indicates a continuation; such as an incomplete list of example items, or a continuation from preceding text.
- **Bold**
  Used to highlight specific terms.
- *Italics*
  Used for emphasis. May also refer to other external documents.

In addition to typographical conventions, the following conventions are used to highlight segments of text:

 A Note box is used to highlight useful or interesting information.

About the Authors

Rob Akershoek, Logicalis SMC (and IT4IT Architect at Shell)

Rob Akershoek is an IT Management Architect and Consultant at Logicalis SMC. For over 20 years he has been involved in improving IT organizations by designing and implementing integrated processes and tools. He has been working on dozens of projects to implement best practices (such as ITIL and COBIT) and responsible for the roll-out of numerous integrated IT management solutions. This included projects related to Enterprise Architecture (EA), Application Portfolio Management (APM), Project Portfolio Management (PPM), Continuous Delivery, Agile and Lean Software Development, Test Management, Deployment Automation, Service Monitoring, IT Service Management (ITSM), Software Asset Management (SAM), IT Financial Management (ITFM), IT Reporting, CMDB, IT Asset Management, and Automated Discovery. Currently he is working as an IT4IT architect at Shell responsible for the solution architecture and design of IT management solutions. In this role he has been involved in The Open Group IT4IT Forum from the start.

Erik Witte, UMBRiO

Erik Witte is Managing Director of UMBRiO and Co-chair of the IT4IT Adoption Work Group within The Open Group IT4IT Forum. He gained insight through more than 15 years of experience from the vendor perspective working for IBM (Tivoli), Oracle, and HP Software. In recent years he founded two companies. The first aimed at implementing IT management solutions and his current company UMBRiO with a strong focus on IT transformation and the creation and adoption of IT management standards.

Etienne Terpstra-Hollander, Hewlett Packard Enterprise

Etienne Terpstra-Hollander is an IT4IT Solution Architect within HPE Software Services, where he is implementing IT4IT for HPE's customers. He is currently working as the IT4IT Design Authority within the Architecture Team of the Netherlands Police's ICT department. He has been working on IT4IT since its birth and was co-author for the original Request-to-Fulfill Value Stream use-case document (at the time called ERP4IT). At the moment he is involved in various workgroups within The Open Group IT4IT Forum.

Trademarks

Amazon® is a registered trademark of Amazon in the US and other countries.

ArchiMate®, DirecNet®, Making Standards Work®, OpenPegasus®, The Open Group®, TOGAF®, UNIX®, and the Open Brand ("X" logo) are registered trademarks and Boundaryless Information Flow™, Build with Integrity Buy with Confidence™, Dependability Through Assuredness™, FACE™, IT4IT™, Open Platform 3.0™, Open Trusted Technology Provider™, and the Open "O" logo and The Open Group Certification logo are trademarks of The Open Group in the United States and other countries.

CMMI® is registered in the US Patent and Trademark Office by Carnegie Mellon University.

COBIT®, ISACA®, ITGI®, and IT Governance Institute® are registered trademarks and Risk IT™ and Val IT™ are trademarks of the Information Systems Audit and Control Association (ISACA) and the IT Governance Institute.

Docker® is a registered trademark of Docker, Inc. in the United States and/or other countries.

Force.com® is a registered trademark of Salesforce.com, Inc.

IT Infrastructure Library®, ITIL®, and PRINCE2® are registered trademarks of AXELOS Limited.

Linux® is a registered trademark of Linus Torvalds.

.NET®, Microsoft®, Windows®, and Windows Azure® are registered trademarks of Microsoft Corporation in the United States and/or other countries.

OMG®, Unified Modeling Language®, and UML®, are registered trademarks of the Object Management Group, Inc. in the United States and/or other countries.

Oracle® and Java® are registered trademarks of Oracle and/or its affiliates.

PMBOK® is a registered trademark of the Project Management Institute, Inc. which is registered in the United States and other nations.

SAP® is a registered trademark of SAP SE in Germany and in several other countries.

SFIA® (Skills for the Information Age) is a registered trademark of the SFIA Foundation Limited.

VMware® is a registered trademark or trademark of VMware, Inc. in the United States and/or other jurisdictions.

All other brands, company, and product names are used for identification purposes only and may be trademarks that are the sole property of their respective owners.

Acknowledgements

The Open Group gratefully acknowledges:

- Past and present members of The Open Group IT4IT Forum for developing the IT4IT Reference Architecture and additional associated materials.
- The following contributors and reviewers:
  - Sam Courtney
  - Michael Fulton
  - Andrew Josey
  - Sylvain Marie
  - Mark Smalley
  - Niels van Barneveld
  - Karel van Zeeland
  - Bart Verbrugge

Referenced Documents

The following documents are referenced in this Management Guide.

(Please note that the links below are good at the time of writing but cannot be guaranteed for the future.)

- Application Services Library, ASL Foundation (2005); retrieved 11/13/2005, from www.aslfoundation.org.
- ArchiMate® 2.1 Specification, Open Group Standard (C13L), December 2013, published by The Open Group; refer to: www.opengroup.org/bookstore/catalog/c13l.htm.
- CMMI for Acquisition, Version 1.3, CMMI Product Team, Pittsburgh PA, Carnegie Mellon Software Engineering Institute (2010).
- CMMI for Development, Version 1.3, CMMI Product Team, Pittsburgh PA, Carnegie Mellon Software Engineering Institute (2010).
- CMMI for Services, Version 1.3, CMMI Product Team, Pittsburgh PA, Carnegie Mellon Software Engineering Institute (2010).
- Control Objectives for Information and Related Technology (COBIT 5), ISACA; refer to www.isaca.org.
- ISO 9000:2015: Quality Management Systems – Fundamentals and Vocabulary; refer to: www.iso.org/iso/home/store/catalogue_tc/catalogue_detail.htm?csnumber=45481.
- ISO 9001:2015: Quality Management Systems – Requirements; refer to: www.iso.org/iso/home/store/catalogue_tc/catalogue_detail.htm?csnumber=62085.
- ISO 21500:2012: Guidance on Project Management; refer to: www.iso.org/iso/catalogue_detail?csnumber=50003.
- ISO 31000:2009: Risk Management – Principles and Guidelines; refer to: www.iso.org/iso/home/store/catalogue_tc/catalogue_detail.htm?csnumber=43170.
- ISO/IEC 16350:2015: Information Technology – Systems and Software Engineering – Application Management; refer to: www.iso.org/iso/catalogue_detail.htm?csnumber=57922.
- ISO/IEC 19770: Information Technology – IT Asset Management.
- ISO/IEC 20000: Information Technology – Service Management.
- ISO/IEC 25010:2011: Systems and Software Engineering – Systems and Software Quality Requirements and Evaluation (SQuaRE) – System and

Software Quality Models; refer to: www.iso.org/iso/home/store/catalogue_tc/catalogue_detail.htm?csnumber=35733.

- ISO/IEC 27000:2014: Information Technology – Security Techniques – Information Security Management Systems – Overview and Vocabulary; refer to: www.iso.org/iso/home/store/catalogue_tc/catalogue_detail.htm?csnumber=63411.

- ISO/IEC 38500:2015: Information Technology – Governance of IT for the Organization; refer to: www.iso.org/iso/home/store/catalogue_tc/catalogue_detail.htm?csnumber=62816.

- ISO/IEC/IEEE 29119: Software and Systems Engineering – Software Testing.

- IT Infrastructure Library (ITIL), AXELOS Limited; refer to: www.axelos.com/best-practice-solutions/itil.

- M. Porter: Competitive Advantage: Creating and Sustaining Superior Performance, ISBN: 978-0684841465, Free Press; 1 Edition (June 1998).

- Project Management Institute: A Guide to the Project Management Body of Knowledge (PMBOK) (2013).

- Rational Unified Process (RUP): Best Practices for Software Development Teams, Rational Software (2011).

- Scaled Agile Framework (SAFe), D. Leffingwell, A. Yakyma et al.; refer to: http://scaledagileframework.com (2014).

- The Open Group IT4IT™ Reference Architecture, Version 2.0, Open Group Standard (C155), October 2015, published by The Open Group; refer to: www.opengroup.org/bookstore/catalog/c155.htm.

- TOGAF® Version 9.1 (English version), Open Group Standard, available online at www.opengroup.org/architecture/togaf9-doc/arch, and also available as TOGAF® Version 9.1 "The Book" (ISBN: 978 90 8753 6794, G116) at www.opengroup.org/bookstore/catalog/g116.htm.

- Unified Modeling Language (UML), Object Management Group (OMG); refer to: www.uml.org.

Chapter 1

Executive Summary

Business is in the middle of an unfolding era of disruption, driven by digital transformation, which challenges how IT is organized and managed today. The role of IT in the business is elevated from being a support function to an enabler to drive innovation, enhance competitive advantage, boost productivity, and reduce cost by applying new innovative technology. However, new technologies, such as big data and cloud, can only provide value to the business if these can be properly implemented and managed. Unfortunately, most IT organizations are not ready to cope with this new demand of IT and are therefore headed for a crisis. More and more IT leaders realize that the current IT operating models are no longer viable and that the IT function needs to reinvent itself. A fundamentally different approach is needed than how we plan, build, deliver, and run IT today.

Despite the availability of many best practices, frameworks, and standards for managing IT, enterprises often suffer from poor services and high costs and risks due to a silo'ed IT function with badly integrated IT management tools. To reinvent IT, the CIOs must go beyond current process-based approaches and equip their teams with the right information and tools to support new ecosystem collaborations, completely automate end-to-end workflows, and provide the business with the controls to govern IT. The Open Group IT4IT Reference Architecture standard with its value-chain-based IT operating model address this problem by providing a prescriptive and detailed information model-based framework that enhances and supports traditional process-based frameworks and standards.

The IT4IT Reference Architecture was created because there is a need for a holistic, concise, and structured standard of how IT should be managed in order to provide maximum value for the business (managing IT as a business) based upon the IT Value Chain.

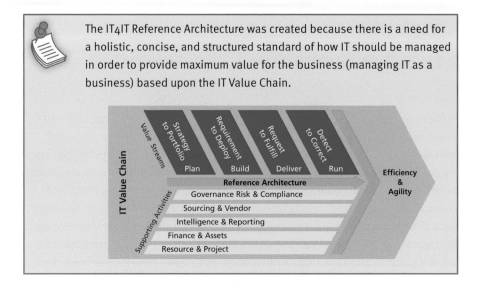

The IT4IT standard is a vendor-neutral open standard for managing the business of IT. It is developed and maintained by The Open Group IT4IT Forum, in which consumer organizations, IT vendors, and academic institutions participate. The standard is designed to be used with process-based frameworks and standards such as ITIL and ISO/IEC 20000 for IT Service Management. While these frameworks and standards place emphasis on process, the IT4IT Reference Architecture focuses on the capabilities and information needed to manage a service through its lifecycle. It defines how the IT function can be supported by information systems automating the IT activities as well as providing the necessary insight to improve IT decision-making and support continuous improvement.

As "IT for IT" implies, it refers to the internal activities and relationships within the IT function of an enterprise. It is about improving the business of IT by using IT as effectively as businesses use IT. The standard enables optimized IT resources (in particular IT management information systems), together with more efficient and controlled IT operations. These IT-related results can be translated into benefits for the enterprise in terms of improvement to the financial bottom line, the risk profile, and to enable the business to enhance its competitive position.

1.1 Benefits

The IT4IT Reference Architecture describes how the new IT function should be managed to optimize the value of IT for the business. Like a business, IT's strategic goal is to create value via IT. This value can come through enabling the business to develop innovative products and/or services, expanding markets (growth strategy), or helping the business become more efficient and cost-effective (productivity).

The IT4IT Reference Architecture enables a more streamlined, transparent, and automated IT function across the entire IT value chain.

Both the enterprise's operating expenditure and capital expenditure are reduced. Operating expenditure is reduced by making both IT operations and business operations more efficient. The improvement in IT development and operations efficiency is realized by improving the information exchange across all parts of the IT function as well as automating IT management tasks. Improving the adaptability of the IT operating model and therefore reducing the impact and cost of changes also reduce IT operating expenditure. The efficiency improvement in business operations is realized by reducing the number and size of IT-related business disruptions, and by accelerated deployment of any IT functionality that improves business operations efficiency. Rationalizing the information systems used to manage and support the IT function reduces capital expenditure. For enterprises with a large IT function, an IT cost reduction of between 5% and 20% is feasible.

The enterprise's risk profile is improved by greater transparency and tighter control of IT services throughout its lifecycle and therefore more predictable costs, delivery, and quality of IT services, leading in turn to more predictable business operations.

Improving business operations, enhancing competitive advantage, and boosting customer loyalty by quicker introduction of new or improved products realize the improvement of the enterprise's revenue. Customer loyalty is improved by more reliable IT services that impact customers directly or indirectly. Products that depend on IT can be launched quicker due to the improved throughput of IT operations.

1.2   Transformation and Reshaping the IT Function

The transformation that is needed to realize these benefits entails adoption of the IT4IT standard. The standard comprises a reference architecture and value chain-based IT operating model for managing the business of IT. The reference architecture and IT operating model cover all of the activities that are needed to provide business functions with appropriate IT services.

The IT4IT Reference Architecture describes the IT function from a value focused end-to-end perspective covering all capabilities and data needed to manage the IT services. It describes the IT function both as IT service provider to the business, and as consumer of IT services that support the IT function. The standard specifies the IT function's workflows, integrations, data, and functions as requirements for (automated) information systems that support the IT function.

The transformation can be undertaken incrementally, enabling the benefits to be realized as soon as possible.

1.3   Target Audience

The IT4IT Reference Architecture is primarily aimed at IT functions within enterprises that rely on large, complex, and changeable information systems, which are supported by multiple internal and external parties. These IT functions can improve the quality and cost of their IT services by adopting the IT4IT value stream approach, and by stipulating that IT tools and IT services comply with the IT4IT interoperability standards.

The IT4IT standard is therefore relevant for not only the enterprise's internal IT function, but also for external tool vendors, IT management improvement consultancies, external IT service providers, external IT component providers, and training and certification providers. Within these organizations, the IT4IT standard should attract the interest of senior managers and their trusted advisors, and those who are tasked with actually improving the "business of IT".

1.4 Complementary with ITIL and Other Frameworks and Standards

The IT4IT Reference Architecture should be used together with other standards and frameworks, such as PMBOK Guide, COBIT, and ITIL for IT Service Management. The IT Value Chain-based IT operating model complements these existing standards and process best practices by combining them into an overarching blueprint, in which Enterprise Architecture, portfolio management, project management, and service development are integrated with IT Service Management, enabling the IT function to be managed from an end-to-end perspective.

The IT4IT Reference Architecture's Service Model, Information Model, Functional Model, and Integration Model add a layer of prescriptive detail to COBIT and ITIL-based processes, providing the IT function with requirements for selecting and implementing interoperable IT solutions that support and automate activities within the IT function. This includes developing more flexible IT processes and IT management solutions and building stronger, more fluid connections among employees and with customers and vendors.

Chapter 2

Introduction

This chapter provides a brief introduction to IT management and the IT4IT Reference Architecture. It highlights the challenges and gaps within the current IT function, builds a case for change, and explains why there is a need to transform the IT organization using the IT4IT value streams and the IT4IT Reference Architecture as an enabler to improve the value of IT for the business.

Topics addressed in this chapter:

- An introduction to IT management, including its challenges and issues. This explains the problem that the IT4IT Reference Architecture is resolving.
- An overview of key demands and drivers for changing the current IT function (to become a service broker and integrator). This explains why the IT4IT approach is important for the new IT organization.
- A high-level introduction to the IT4IT standard explaining the IT4IT value streams and IT4IT Reference Architecture. These are both described in detail in Chapter 3.
- The positioning of the IT4IT standard *versus* other industry best practices and standards such as ITIL, explaining how the IT4IT approach is complementary to existing best practices.

2.1   What is IT Management (and IT4IT)?

The IT function needs to be managed similar to the business having its own value chain, processes, and information systems. IT4IT (or IT for the IT function) refers to all the capabilities you need to manage IT services throughout its entire lifecycle. Similar to the business using IT to support or automate its business processes, the IT organization uses IT to support and automate IT management processes. This includes information systems such as a Project Portfolio Management (PPM) system, development and testing tools, a Configuration Management Database (CMDB), or an IT Service Management (ITSM) system for managing incidents, problems, and changes. All these IT management tools represent "IT for the IT organization", therefore referred to as IT4IT. The IT organization is becoming more dependent upon these information systems to automate IT management activities such as build, test, deploy, monitor, and perform automated recovery. Due to the growing importance of IT management to demonstrate the value of IT, but also due to its increase in complexity, there is need to acquire new skills and competences within the IT organization to deliver these integrated IT4IT solutions.

IT needs to be managed; it will not take care of itself ...
The essential principle behind the IT4IT approach is that the IT function should be organized and managed as a business. Similar to the business, it has its own value chain (and processes) and therefore needs its own information systems or tools to support these processes. The challenge is that the IT function has never been constructed with an overarching design and vision in mind. The IT function has typically been organized and over and over again reorganized through a series of *ad hoc*, chaotic, and fragmented initiatives. So far, the IT organization has got away with it, but now, due to higher demands and new technology trends, the IT function is stretched beyond the limits of its traditional competences. The new IT function needs to reorganize itself around the IT Value Chain.

Figure 1 illustrates the positioning of the business, IT, and "IT4IT" within the IT function. IT4IT in this diagram refers to the function that provides the IT management standard practices, processes, and tools.

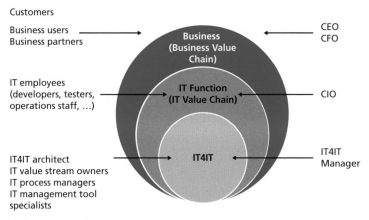

Figure 1: IT4IT within the IT Function

The business consumes IT services, delivered by the IT function, for various goals such as to automate business processes, enable business innovation, improve decision-making, and/or to optimize communication and collaboration with all involved parties in the value chain such as suppliers, business partners, and customers. IT is even becoming part of business services that are directly delivered to the customers; for example, online banking, mobile applications, and a web shop to order products and provide customer support.

Table 1: IT for Business *versus* IT for the IT Function

	IT for the Business	**IT for the IT Organization (IT4IT)**
Customer/User	• Business and its customers	• IT organization and its customers (business)
Value Chain Primary Processes (examples)	• Design of products, services, or processes • Marketing and sales • Production • Logistics/distribution • Customer service	• Service Portfolio Management • Project Portfolio Management (PPM) • Service Design and Development • Release and Deployment Management • Request Fulfillment • Change Management • Service Monitoring • Incident Management • ...
Supporting Processes	• HR Management • Procurement and Vendor Management • Financial Management • Information Technology (IT) • ...	• HR Management • Procurement and Vendor Management • Financial Management (for IT) • Configuration and IT Asset Management • ...
Value Streams (examples)	• Idea to Market • Make to Order • Order to Cash • Manufacturing to Distribution • Recruitment to Retirement • ...	• Strategy to Portfolio • Requirement to Deploy • Request to Fulfill • Detect to Correct

	IT for the Business	IT for the IT Organization (IT4IT)
IT Services/ Applications (examples of information systems)	• Product Lifecycle Management (PLM) • CRM system • Enterprise Resource Planning (ERP) system • HR system • …	• Project Portfolio Management (PPM) • Development and Test Management Tools (ALM) • IT Service Management (ITSM) system • Configuration Management Database (CMDB) • Identity and Access Management (IAM) system • Service monitoring tools • Security management information systems • …
Generic Services	• Document and content management • Collaboration and communication systems • HR system • Financial Management System • …	

The IT function (represented by the IT organization) embodies all departments and teams responsible for developing and operating IT services – including external service providers from which services are sourced. The IT organization manages the entire lifecycle of all these IT services; such as the customer-facing web shop, a CRM system, or HR system. The IT organization acts as a service broker and integrator responsible for the design, development, deployment, operations, and continuous improvement of all IT services and applications delivered to the business. To deliver these services, the IT organization typically relies on work performed by an increasing number of external IT service providers such as technology vendors, hosting providers, cloud vendors, and other managed service providers.

The IT4IT standard describes all capabilities consisting of processes, tools, data, and its integrations to support the IT function, and collaboration with its stakeholders such as the business, system integrators, and external IT service providers.

The IT organization needs to perform wide-ranging activities to plan, build, deliver, and manage IT services. Table 2 provides an example of what IT management is all about – illustrating the complexity of managing IT.

Table 2: Illustrating the Complexity of Processes, Data, and Tools for Managing IT

Examples of IT Processes and Activities to be Executed in the IT Organization	Examples of Data to be Managed in an IT Organization	Examples of Information Systems Needed to Run IT
• Interface with Enterprise Architecture (EA) • Business Relationship Management (BRM) • Service portfolio management • Demand management • Financial management (for IT services) • Requirements management • Service design • Service development • Availability management • Capacity management • Information Security Management (ISMS) • Service validation and testing (or test management) • Service asset and configuration management • IT service continuity management • Business continuity management • Release and deployment management	• IT services and applications • IT roadmaps • Service reviews • Service improvement plans • IT standards and policies • Business demands • Projects (and project plans, project issues, and project costs) • Portfolio backlog item • Requirements (including themes, epics, user stories) • Product and release backlog • Service designs • Development tasks • Sprint and release plans • Source code • Test plans and test cases • Defects • Release • Deployment packages (and run books) • Change and release schedule • Events	• Enterprise Architecture (EA) system • Service (and application) portfolio management system • Policy management system • Project Portfolio Management (PPM) system • Development tools (such as prototyping, requirements engineering, IDE, …) • Test management system • Security test tools • Load/stress testing tools • Deployment and release automation tool • Service catalog • Request management system • Self-service portal • Information Security Management (ISMS) system • Monitoring system • Operations data analytic tools • Diagnostics tools • Run book automation (or IT process automation) • Event management system

Examples of IT Processes and Activities to be Executed in the IT Organization	Examples of Data to be Managed in an IT Organization	Examples of Information Systems Needed to Run IT
• Service monitoring • Event management • Incident management • Problem management • Change management • Request fulfillment • Access management • IT operations management • Service reporting • Continuous improvement (service improvement management) • IT Governance, Risk, and Compliance (GRC) management • Supplier management • Contract management • HR management (for IT) including skills and competence management • (and more)	• Monitoring data such as availability and performance data • Continuity plans • Incident • Problem • Known error • Knowledge items • Documents • Change • Service request • IT risks • Security events and vulnerabilities • IT costs and IT budgets • Configuration items (and IT assets) • SLA and contracts • Licenses • Users (and user identities and access rights) • Capacity plans • Service reports • Continuous improvement register • (and many more)	• Incident and problem management system • Change management system • Business intelligence/ reporting tools • Document management system • Operations management tools (such as backup/ restore tools, job scheduling, element managers) • Information risk management system • CMDB • Discovery and automated inventory • Software Asset Management (SAM) system • Identity and Access Management (IAM) tools • Customer survey tools • Auditing tools • Contract management system • Financial management system • (and many more)

The IT function is becoming dependent on automated tools to support IT management activities and to provide better information to improve decision-making. This requires a unified IT management system supporting the entire IT Value Chain, consisting of IT processes, IT tools, and IT management data. Unfortunately there is not a single tool or vendor that is best-in-class at all the required IT management capabilities. As a result, the IT organization typically needs to select, implement, and integrate many different IT management tools to enable full control over IT. It is not uncommon for an IT organization to have over 100 or more IT management tools.

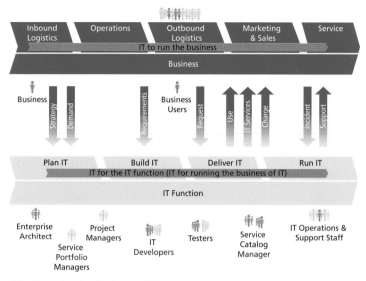

Figure 2: IT for Managing the Business of IT

The IT4IT approach needs to provide all of the necessary IT management capabilities to the different IT workers involved in the IT service lifecycle covering planning, build, delivery, and run activities. The users of IT4IT therefore include all IT stakeholders such as the CIO, IT managers, enterprise architects, project managers, service managers, developers, testers, operations and support staff, team leaders, security specialists, service desk agents, and so on.

Who are the users of IT4IT applications?

IT4IT refers to all the necessary IT management capabilities needed to manage the entire lifecycle of all IT services. Therefore, all employees involved in managing IT are the primary users of IT4IT applications (or IT management tools). However, the business also uses IT4IT applications; for example, to request IT services from the catalog.

All IT workers such as the CIO, IT managers, enterprise architects, PMO office, project managers, demand managers, service managers, developers, testers, service desk agents, license managers, operations staff, and so on are users of IT4IT services. These employees use the IT

management functionality implemented with IT management tools such
as a Project Portfolio Management (PPM) system, a development or
testing tool, the CMDB, or a service desk system.

In addition to IT employees, the business users also use IT4IT
applications. Think about services such as browsing through a service
catalog, requesting IT services (access to a business application, ordering
a new laptop or additional software), or viewing IT costs. Some business
users are also involved in requirements review and test management
activities (such as User Acceptance Testing (UAT)) and use IT4IT
functionality for these purposes.

2.2   IT Management Challenges

We are entering the digital era where the line between "business" and "IT" is
blurring. Technology is increasingly integrated with business processes and
directly affects the customer and business experience. IT no longer just supports
the business; it is becoming an integral part of the business. In order to compete
in the service economy, IT must change from a technology and project-centric
orientation to a new service-centric ecosystem. It must be oriented around
"systems of engagement" that are focused on connecting people in new ways and
creating new experiences and innovation opportunities.

IT is a bureaucratic black-box

The business often perceives the IT function as a black box that they
cannot control; it is seen as bureaucratic, lacking focus, overly complex,
and considered very expensive and slow in responding to business
needs. The IT function is not very transparent and its collaboration (and
communication) with the business are very poor.

Both business and IT executives realize that there is a lot of "waste"
and "slack" in the IT organization and that there is definitively room for
significant improvements. However, they struggled to find the right model
to redesign and transform their IT function.

The IT organization is under constant pressure to provide more cost
transparency (and reduce costs), deliver solutions faster, respond to security

risks, consolidate and rationalize (and standardize) the IT infrastructure, and much more. Corporate IT budgets are constrained while technology demand keeps increasing. Many organizations have already gone through many rounds of change programs, mergers, centralizations and consolidations, outsourcing (and insourcing), new IT strategies, or new management. The organization usually has been stretched beyond its limits.

Key expectations of the business posed to the IT organization are as follows:
- IT understanding the business processes and outcomes, and how IT impacts the business.
- Enable the business to become more innovative, improve customer experience, and support new business models (realizing the digital enterprise).
- Alignment of IT service delivery to business strategy and dynamic business demand, proactively suggesting innovations for the business.
- IT using business terms for benefits, costs, and risks, not "geek speak" about technology components and features.
- Continuously react to business change without being surprised that things change.
- Optimize the return on investment in IT.
- Replace "technical" SLAs by simple, honest, and meaningful reporting.
- Increase the transparency of IT to the business (manage IT from a business perspective).
- Reduce time-to-market to implement new requirements for new or modified services; or to fix problems/vulnerabilities.
- Improve the quality of IT services (to meet the expected service levels).
- Reduce the cost of ownership of IT services throughout the entire lifecycle (lower unit costs).
- Ensure continuous operations reducing business disruptions of failing IT.
- Create a more flexible consumption model for using IT services (instead of having a large amount of investment and fixed costs).
- Respond to new disruptive technologies such as mobility, cloud, big data, and Internet of Things (IoT).
- Control compliance and risks of the delivery of IT services to the business.

In summary, the IT organization needs to become faster, better, cheaper, and more controlled; or, in other words, credible, competitive, predictable, and affordable. In addition, the IT department is expected to be more responsive to innovation and embrace new IT technologies for business use such as mobility, cloud, big data, IoT, and Software-Defined anything (SDx). The following list summarizes a number of these new technology trends that the IT function needs to address:

- Cloud computing; e.g., IaaS, PaaS, and SaaS (and managing hybrid environments)
- Converged infrastructures
- Big data (for use in business intelligence)
- Mobility (e.g., mobile app store)
- IT consumerization
- Bring Your Own Device (BYOD)
- Internet of Things (embedded systems)
- Service-Oriented Architectures (SOA) and Microservices
- Containerization
- Software-Defined Networking (SDN), Software-Defined Data Center (or even more Software-Defined everything)
- Bimodal IT
- Infrastructure as code
- Design thinking
- API economy
- Robotic automation of business processes
- And all other disruptive technologies that are coming next …

However, most IT teams' skills lie in development and operations of legacy systems, leaving many unable to adapt to best serve a constantly changing business environment. This opens the door for the business to adopt shadow-IT, where complexity is mostly only increasing for the IT organization in the initial phases of this adoption. It can even result in complete outplacement of IT all together.

 Today's IT organization faces a clear imperative:
- Manage IT as a business
- Enable the digital transformation of the business
- Provide full transparency on value, costs, and risks of IT services
- Provide more flexible consumption and usage models (more variable IT costs)
- Focus on delivery of end-to-end IT services through value streams (reducing bottlenecks and improving flows)
- Reduce IT costs (lower unit costs) while IT consumption will grow exponentially

- Create a culture of collaboration, innovation, and continuous improvement
- Deliver faster (and become more responsive to business needs)
- Enable new business and drive innovation (to become more competitive and agile)
- Better alignment of IT to achieve business objectives
- Buy before build; using standard market services (such as SaaS) by becoming a broker and integrator of IT services delivered by external vendors
- Build a flexible IT ecosystem brokering and orchestrating services from various external IT service providers
- Adopt a Lean and Agile approach focused on delivering value and high quality services
- Provide more flexibility to continually adapt to changing business environments (this includes elastic infrastructure platforms, flexible cost models, adjustable sourcing options, and so on)
- Enhance customer experience
- Improve security and risk control
- Bridge the skills gap (supply qualified IT professionals for modern IT skills)
- Create a climate of technology experimentation
- Establish new technology architectures that provide more flexibility and scalability
- Implement the right controls to ensure predictable outcomes

More often organizations realize that the current IT function is not very well organized and managed. The IT organization is regarded as bureaucratic with long lead times and many different inefficient controls. The management capabilities of the IT organization and its management tools are typically lagging behind. The timely adoption of new technologies introduces challenges because the required IT management capabilities are not developed. A recent example is the introduction of cloud technologies in many organizations. The use of cloud services is growing fast, but the capability to manage this new cloud environment properly is still immature. Figure 3 highlights this growing gap of new demand for IT *versus* the capability of the IT function to manage this new IT estate.

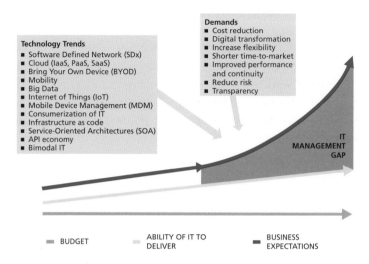

Figure 3: Growing Capability Gap within the IT Function

The IT organization will need to change its IT operating model in such a way that more and more (if not all) services need or can be consumed as market services from the cloud. An increasing number of organizations have defined cloud as the primary delivery method. This again creates new challenges to the IT organization, specifically related to the orchestration and collaboration with an ever-growing number of external service providers to ensure end-to-end delivery to the business. This requires the IT organization to adopt an additional role, one of a service broker. This is illustrated in Figure 4.

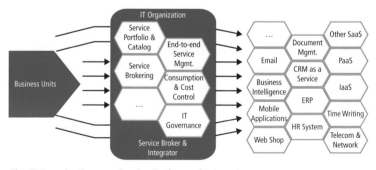

Figure 4: The IT Organization as a Service Broker and Integrator

IT organizations must reinvent themselves and transition into becoming Lean and Agile service providers. They have experimented with Continuous Delivery, DevOps, or any other practice that is promoted by the IT industry. However, what is typically forgotten or not well engineered is how this new IT organization will work across the silos, how it must be equipped with the right IT management tools, and how to make sure that the right information is available to support IT management activities. For example, questions that need to be answered are:

- How can we simplify and rationalize our IT service portfolio?
- How do we align the service portfolio with business strategy and plans? How can we adapt to continuous changing business demands?
- How can we contain IT costs while the consumption and usage of IT will grow significantly?
- How can we become a service broker and integrator, sourcing IT services from external service providers (consume standard market services)?
- How can we become more agile and deliver new functionality faster?
- How can we integrate with the increasing number of vendors (or service providers) such as IaaS, PaaS, and SaaS vendors?
- How can we balance the cost of keeping-the-lights-on *versus* change and innovation?
- How can we improve cost transparency (and reduce costs)?
- How should we deliver and manage new technologies to enable business innovation?
- How can IT enable digital leadership for the business?
- How can we reduce technology debt (legacy technologies, outdated and unsupported versions)?
- How do customers experience the delivery of IT services?
- How can we really harvest the benefits of cloud services?
- How do we manage cloud services (such as PaaS and SaaS)? What do we still need to perform ourselves? What new controls are needed?
- How can we provide self-service capabilities and support the end-to-end workflow from request to fulfillment?
- How can we automate end-to-end workflows/value streams (to reduce the number of manual activities)?
- How can we implement new paradigms such as DevOps and Continuous Delivery?
- How do we ensure all required information is available to support decision-making?

- How can we cope with the increasing risks such as security attacks and responding faster to security vulnerabilities?
- How can we ensure continuous operations for the business (that becomes more dependent upon IT)?
- How can we fill the IT skill (and competence) gap that has undermined our ability to innovate and improve the IT function?

This all comes down to a solid IT management system, bringing IT processes, tools, data, and people (and their skills, attitudes, mind sets) together in a standard IT operating model (using the IT4IT Reference Architecture as guidance).

Summarizing the above: it becomes clear that the IT organization is under enormous pressure to improve transparency, reduce cost, and provide more reliable services, while at the same time provide more innovation and enable new technologies to create new value for the business. IT must become an enabler to support the business in meeting the overall company goals.

The issue is that the current IT operating models are not suitable for the new role that the IT function needs to play. There is an enormous gap that needs to be bridged. To understand this gap in more detail it is important to understand how the IT function is currently managed. One of the core problems is that IT is not managed from an end-to-end perspective – but rather along silos, different technologies, teams, tools, and processes. Business customers are often brought into the process at different points, resulting in miss-set expectations and priorities. This results in a suboptimal management model, as illustrated in Figure 5.

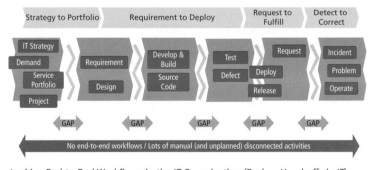

Figure 5: Lacking End-to-End Workflows in the IT Organization (Broken Hand-offs in IT)

IT service delivery suffers from disorganized handovers from business to the IT function and from development to operations. The IT Value Chain is managed through fragmented teams, processes, and tools. An end-to-end IT service view is missing which results in poor transparency and traceability, and that causes higher costs, higher risks, and lower quality. This way of working is blocking the IT organization from making a step change. Typically, different teams or process owners select and implement their own tools; optimizing their own processes without any understanding of the impact on the entire value stream.

Fragmented IT management data repositories/Lacking a common IT information model

The IT organization typically lacks a single system of record to find all relevant IT information. Today many different fragmented repositories exist in which IT data is maintained. A common data model for IT has been lacking for many years. Some examples of IT data relevant for the IT function are shown in the table below.

Example of Data Managed in the IT Function			
• Business process (and business services) • Demand (or idea) • Incident • License • User manuals • Service catalog items • Project risks • IT risks • Event • IT skills and competences • Service reports • Business Impact Assessments (BIA) • Builds	• Business capabilities • Investment • Problem • Contract • IT operating procedures • Requirements (themes, epics, user stories) • Project issues • Policies • Availability data • IT training plans • Customer surveys • Known errors • Deployment or release packages	• IT service (or application) or products • Business goals and drivers • Change • Time sheet • Knowledge items • Sprint and release plans • Audit findings • IT standards • Capacity and performance data • IT organization structure • Design specifications • Improvement opportunities • Run books • Capacity plan	• Roadmap • Project (and related benefits and business case) • Configuration item • Project document • Service request • Project plan • Security incidents • End-of-life or end-of-support data • Application logs • IT roles and responsibilities • Invoices (from IT suppliers) • Source codes • Test plan • SLA (and other contracts)

• Test cases
• Suppliers (or
  vendor data)
• Access rights
• IT budget
	• Defects
	• Locations
	• Installed
	  software
	• Vendor
	  information
		• Identities (or
		  users)
		• Hardware assets
		• IT costs
			• Subscriptions of
			  users to IT services
			• IT cost centers
			  (and WBSE)
			• Service KPIs,
			  metrics, and
			  service reports

The IT administration of the average IT organization has a large number of gaps, considering:

• There is no single repository containing all IT services and applications (and its related technologies).
• There is no insight into which projects are planned (or in-flight) for the IT services and applications in the portfolio.
• The total cost of ownership of IT services is not transparent (for example, infrastructure costs, contract and license costs, support FTE).
• Requirements are not correctly captured and managed (not traceable).
• The CMDB is not up-to-date and a lot of configuration data is missing (for example, what applications are using what IT resources).
• There is no repository to manage all subscriptions of users to IT services, applications, and IT resources (identity and access administration).
• There is a lack of data related to usage, performance, and availability of IT services from a business perspective.
• Documents cannot be easily found (for example, latest design documents, user guides, and so on).
• A large amount of changes and incidents are not formally registered in the IT Service Management (ITSM) system.
• Licenses purchased, actual software usage, and compliance are unknown (no solid SAM administration).
• Contracts are managed by using spreadsheets. Contracts with vendors are not related to the services and assets provided by these vendors.

As a result, an IT organization typically doesn't know what applications are running on which servers, who is using them, what it costs, what licenses have been purchased, how the application is performing, what capacity or IT resources are needed to run the application, who owns the application, which suppliers support them, when the contract ends or needs to be renewed.

A lot of productivity is lost by having IT employees spending time searching for information, updating the wrong version of a document, disturbing other colleagues, waiting for the data, and creating their own reports (or version of the truth), or due to the frustration of not having access to accurate and complete data. In other cases, there is just too much information that is not relevant any more or even incorrect (as it cannot be maintained).

IT data is spread across many different systems and repositories each having its own data model. As a result, information is not easily available to support decision-making. It is very difficult to find the relevant information. In addition, the ownership of data is unclear and data quality is questionable.

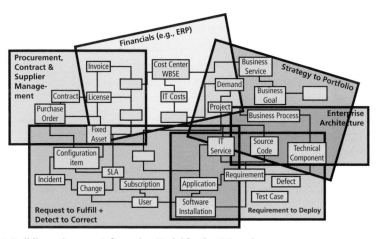

Figure 6: Building a Common Information Model for the IT Function

It should not be a surprise, looking at how IT is organized today, that the business raises concerns such as: "Why does it cost so much?", "Why does it take so long?", or even "Why is it so hard to work with IT and why can't we get what we want?".

The following list provides examples of key symptoms indicating gaps and issues with the current IT management environment:
• The presence of a complex IT management tooling landscape with many different management tools, data repositories, and interfaces (or, conversely, a near-total lack of IT management tools)

- Lacking cost transparency of IT service delivery (and the IT resources consumed when delivering a service)
- Different support teams having their own tools (they select and implement their own)
- The existence of many customizations and homegrown tools (for example, a proprietary web shop for ordering IT services)
- High workload and stress for IT specialists (with business complaints that their priority items are not addressed on time)
- The lack of an integrated IT service catalog
- Large amount of unplanned (or *ad hoc* or emergency) activities
- No single repository with the entire service/application portfolio (defining the IT portfolio)
- Lack of standard integrations with different external service providers
- No adequate information available to support the decision-making process (or a lot of effort to find relevant information)
- IT administrations are not up-to-date (for example, the CMDB, license, and contract management)
- Most IT activities are still performed through manual procedures (limited use of automation)
- No agreed unified IT management architecture
- No formal ownership in the IT organization for the IT tools and its IT data; ownership is fragmented around different departments and teams, each developing their own processes, practices, and tools
- A huge amount of waste; for example, due to rework and over-capacity (or underutilized IT resources and licenses)
- High costs to maintain and implement IT management tools
- There are many administration gaps in IT (for example, what licenses have been bought, what applications are deployed, who is using them, and so on)
- Difficult to find information and data to support decision-making
- Cumbersome integration with external suppliers and between tools; complex interfaces between IT management tools
- No consolidated self-service portal to interact with the IT organization (instead there many different unclear channels to order, report incidents, ask for help, etc.)
- No clear communication with the business in case of outages or planned new releases
- No plug-and-play of IT tools from different vendors
- A lot of data and (manually created) reports but not much insight

- Heavy dependency upon email and spreadsheets to manage IT activities and performance as well as the trusted data source – it seems like the IT is managed using spreadsheets

To make things even worse, there are a number of other trends that make the IT management capabilities even more important, such as:
- Increasing number of IT services or applications (such as micro-services, mobile applications)
- Increase in consumption of IT resources (such as storage, number of transactions)
- More changes and releases (due to incremental and continuous delivery)
- Increasing volume of events and machine data
- Increasing number of security risks, cyber attacks, and vulnerabilities that need to be mitigated
- More devices connected to the network (such as IoT, BYOD)
- More service requests to continuously act upon changing workload and consumption volumes
- More and more frequent changes in the business (such as mergers, acquisitions, disinvestments, reorganizations, etc.)

Characteristics of a new IT operating model:
- Implement end-to-end value streams to focus on delivering value to the business; and apply Lean and Agile practices focused on business outcomes
- Provide standard IT management capabilities consisting of integrated processes, tools, and data
- Automate IT management activities as much as possible to eliminate manual activities, reduce errors, deliver faster, reduce waste, more predictable, etc.
- Implement the service broker and integrator role of sourcing, orchestrating, and integrating standard market services
- Provide self-service capabilities (business-led IT) to the business and IT
- Ensure IT specialists have all information and data available to support their work and make the right decisions
- Support new organizational structures that empower IT specialists and create a less bureaucratic environment
- Adopt new management paradigms such as Agile, Bimodal IT, DevOps, Lean IT, and Continuous Delivery

- Provide transparency and insight to support the continuous improvement of the IT function
- Support new collaboration technologies to optimize communication between all stakeholders involved in the IT Value Chain
- Business-oriented service management delivering IT as a service

As a result, the IT organization needs to do more – and coordinate more than ever before. This in turn means there is a need to automate IT processes. Thought leaders realize that a fundamentally different approach is needed to create, organize, and manage the new IT paradigm. This new approach should be based upon end-to-end value streams, which are in contrast to the currently used, often-fragmented process and tool approach. The new approach is characterized by:

- An end-to-end IT Value Chain – The important theme of the IT4IT approach is that the entire plan-to-operations lifecycle must be viewed as one end-to-end value chain composed of individual value streams. Individual methodologies can be followed for individual segments (value streams) or that processes (such as SCRUM on one end and ITIL on the other, so long as those processes can be plugged together) form a unified process which, in turn, can be managed from a unified point-of-view.
- Integrated and rationalized tooling landscape – The IT4IT standard defines a structured approach for collaboration and automation. Support themes such as "infrastructure as code", "model or topology-driven automation", and "continuous deployment" are all concepts that would fall under the IT4IT approach.
- Common information model – The IT4IT standard defines a common information model for the data and metrics needed to manage IT.
- Supplier integration – Ability to orchestrate and coordinate IT service delivery amongst the many service providers.

The next section provides a more detailed introduction of the IT4IT value streams and the IT4IT Reference Architecture.

2.3 An Introduction to The Open Group IT4IT Reference Architecture Standard

The IT4IT Reference Architecture standard comprises an architecture and value chain-based operating model for managing the business of IT. The operating model defined by the standard serves the digital enterprise with support for real-world use-cases (e.g., cloud-sourcing, software-defined datacenter, Agile, DevOps, and service brokering) as well as embracing and complementing existing process frameworks and methodologies (e.g., ITIL, COBIT, SAFe, and the TOGAF standard).

The IT4IT Reference Architecture provides a prescriptive framework to support the value chain-based IT operating model and service-centric management ecosystem. Think of it as describing all information you need to run and optimize IT, defining the automation you need to support end-to-end value streams, and the standard and open integrations with the external service providers. The IT4IT Reference Architecture also provides a standard blueprint of all IT solutions needed for managing a modern IT organization.

It offers great value to any company that takes managing the business of IT seriously, and especially those with an interest in business and IT transitions. It allows the IT function within an organization to achieve the same level of business discipline, predictability, and efficiency as other functions in the business.

The standard is focused on defining, sourcing, consuming, and managing IT services by looking holistically at the entire IT Value Chain. While existing frameworks and standards have placed their main emphasis on process, this standard is process-agnostic, focused instead on the information (or information systems) and automation to manage a service through its lifecycle. It describes the functional components (IT management software) that are required to produce and consume the data. Once integrated together, a system of record fabric for IT management is created that ensures full visibility and traceability of the service from cradle to grave.

The IT4IT Reference Architecture is built around the concept of a value chain. The IT Value Chain is the series of activities that IT performs to add value to a business service or IT service.

What is a value chain?

A sequence of activities required to design, produce, and provide a specific good or service, and along which information, materials, and worth flows.

(For more on the value chain concept, refer to Michael Porter's "Competitive Advantage: Creating and Sustaining Superior Performance".)

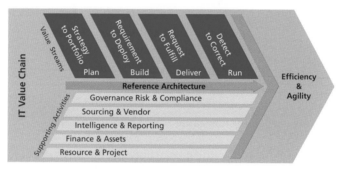

Figure 7: The IT Value Chain

Each value stream is centered on an essential element of the Service Model and the constellation of key data objects (Information Model) and functional components (Functional Model) that support it. Together, the four value streams play a vital role in helping IT holistically manage the full service lifecycle:

- The **Strategy to Portfolio (S2P) Value Stream** receives demand for a new or significantly improved service from the business and develops the Conceptual Service Blueprint to represent the new or enhanced business/IT service that is requested. The Conceptual Service Blueprint is the bridge between business and IT in that it provides the business context for the service along with the high-level architectural attributes.

- The **Requirement to Deploy (R2D) Value Stream** consumes the Conceptual Service Blueprint and triggers service design work. This results in the creation (or modification) of the Logical Service Model that contains more detailed requirements that describe more technical aspects of the service. The R2D Value Stream is where sourcing, development, builds, tests, and releases are created, resulting in a deployable service (expressed as the Service Release Blueprint data object).

- The **Request to Fulfill (R2F) Value Stream** receives the Logical Service Blueprint after it has gone through development, test, and release approval. For repeatedly consumable services, the R2F Value Stream transitions the service into production and makes it consumable for its users. Also it creates a Service Catalog Entry.
- The **Detect to Correct (D2C) Value Stream** is engaged and begins monitoring once a new service is put into production and when the business requests another instance of a service in the Service Catalog to create and manage the Physical or Realized Service Model. This is the Physical Service Model that contains information used in the creation of a service instance (realized service) such as technology and platform choices, locations, configuration settings, and supplier requirements.

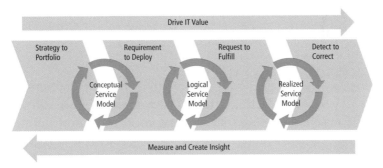

Figure 8: IT4IT Value Streams and Service Models

Each value stream encapsulates the capabilities that are necessary to manage the service lifecycle. These capabilities are realized as a set of functional components and data objects.

A functional component is basically a software building block (or IT management tool). It represents the smallest unit of technology that can stand on its own and be useful as a whole to an IT practitioner (or IT service provider). Functional components must have defined inputs and outputs that are data objects and they must have an impact on a key data object. Data objects represent tangible, non-trivial data items that are owned, consumed, produced, or modified by functional components. Key functional components drive core activities within a value stream.

A functional component can be supported by (or automated with) one or more IT management tools; but one tool can also support multiple functional components. The challenge is to select and implement a portfolio of IT management tools that optimize the activities and integrations provided by the functional components within the IT4IT Reference Architecture.

2.4   Why Use the IT4IT Reference Architecture?

The IT4IT standard is for those organizations that realize a fundamentally different approach is needed for managing the new IT. The new IT organization is characterized by sourcing and orchestrating IT services from many internal and external service providers such as cloud vendors. The current fragmented approach of ownership of processes, tools, data, and controls inhibits continuous improvement and prevents IT from performing its new role as a transparent and added-value business partner.

The new IT organization also relies more on automation of IT activities supporting these end-to-end processes. Unfortunately, there is not a single tool (or solution) or best practice that covers all IT management capabilities needed to run an IT organization as a business. Therefore, we need to carefully select IT management tools and best practices to be implemented in the IT organization. To equip and empower the IT employees with the right set of tools (to automate end-to-end workflows) and provide information to support decision-making, a blueprint or reference architecture is required defining how to manage the business of IT. This integrated model supports the IT4IT value streams that are needed to significantly improve the performance of IT and to facilitate the transition to a Lean, Agile, and streamlined IT operating model supporting a new multi-vendor IT ecosystem. This is in contrast to how IT management has been executed up to now, which was basically an unplanned and *ad hoc* approach to implement IT management tools and IT processes.

 The adoption of the IT4IT standard is not just a reboot of your IT organization, nor a service pack, patch, or fix, nor an upgrade, but rather a reinvention of IT management. The IT4IT approach powers the IT organization with automated workflows, empowers the IT workers, and provides the business the instruments to control IT. The business controls IT through self-service portals while the IT organization controls the performance of its suppliers through improved visibility.

Traditionally, the implementation of IT management solutions required a large amount of configuration and customization before these tools could actually be used within the IT organization. IT tool vendors have long been offering proprietary solutions for specific functions within the IT Value Chain, but without any real standards for integration. Although IT management tool vendors and IT organizations use best practices and standards such as ITIL, the actual implementation varies considerable between organizations, and interoperability between tools is still cumbersome. There are still a lot of detailing and design choices to be made before ITIL can be operationalized and supported by automated tools. As a result, IT organizations are forced to build these themselves in isolation and typically at huge cost. This is simply unsustainable given the increased move towards cloud and outsourcing providers, and is a problem that the IT industry as a whole needs to fix. This traditional approach often results in a complex mesh of products and solutions requiring countless point-to-point integrations to accommodate the variations in process.

Instead, four pillars anchor the IT4IT Reference Architecture approach for the IT Value Chain:
- The Service Model, defining how services should be managed in the portfolio
- The Information Model, defining what information we need to operate IT
- The Functional Model, defining the IT management systems we need to automate and support IT activities
- The Integration Model, defining how processes, data, and systems need to be connected to deliver value to the business

These pillars, when captured and modeled correctly, remain constant regardless of changes to process, technology, and/or capabilities.

The goal of the IT4IT standard is to guide the improvement of the entire IT management capability of an IT organization using a value chain approach. Most CIOs and IT managers have realized that losing sight of the big picture due to the imminent urge of the daily details is blocking them from improving the IT function. Instead of improving specific processes, tools, or information needs, the focus should be on improving the system as a whole.

The easiest way to lose sight of the big picture is to focus on details. Most IT organizations manage their IT in different silos, each responsible for their own processes and tools. As a result, we lack an end-to-end view into the performance, value, risks, and costs of IT services.

*"**Gartner research** suggests that many IT functions are struggling to contain IT cost. Many companies see base cost (run and maintain of the estate) going up, leaving less funds available for innovation and new business applications. The insights that IT4IT promises to deliver will enable opportunities for cost reduction to be identified, freeing up funding for innovation. Gartner estimates that for a $1B per annum IT function, this benefit could be 5%-20% of total budget."*

Figure 9: Quote from Val Sribar, Group Vice-President, Gartner Enterprise Software Research Group

Use of the IT4IT Reference Architecture will:

- Provide the capabilities for managing the business of IT that enable IT execution across the entire IT Value Chain in a better, faster, and more cost-effective manner, while reducing risks
- Reduce expenditure on IT management tooling by using tools that are IT4IT compliant and therefore easier to integrate
- Increase resilience and efficiency in operations by better information provisioning and a higher degree of automation
- Increase agility in development by providing quicker and better feedback
- Increase throughput from development to operations by providing an end-to-end framework
- Reduce risk and therefore increase predictability by providing more comprehensive information about assets and activities across the whole value chain
- Reduce costs, management attention, and staff disruption associated with reorganization by using an inherently stable IT operating model
- Optimize investments in new IT services for the business by better insight into the capabilities of the current information systems
- Provide to ability to continuously improve IT services by providing improved information and insight in IT performance
- Provide improved interoperability, collaboration, and orchestration across the new multi-sourced ecosystem by having standards to enable seamless integration

- Provide a complete holistic IT4IT solution for managing the business of IT by leveraging existing standards and best practices

2.5 Relationship with ITIL and Other Practices or Standards

There are many different best practices, frameworks, and standards related to IT management such as ITIL, COBIT, PMBOK, PRINCE2, ISO/IEC 20000, ASL, BiSL, to mention a few. While these best practices and frameworks have placed emphasis on process, the IT4IT standard is process-agnostic, focusing on how the IT function can be automated and supported by the right information (or data) to do the work. In addition, the IT4IT Reference Architecture provides the bigger picture of how IT services should be managed, throughout the entire lifecycle, by looking holistically at the entire IT Value Chain.

 Despite the existence of so many different best practices, guidelines, standards, and reference models, none of them provide the complete picture of what is needed to manage the entire IT service lifecycle (and IT Value Chain). The IT4IT Reference Architecture provides this holistic view, as well as the prescriptive details of how to support the IT function with automated IT management tools, using a common information model.

Figure 10: IT4IT Filling the Gaps in the Current Market of Standards, Best Practices, and Frameworks

ITIL and COBIT are the most commonly used process-oriented best practice frameworks for IT management. Both describe a broad range of processes and activities to be performed by the IT function throughout the service lifecycle. However, ITIL does not cover all processes and activities within the IT function, such as Enterprise Architecture, Project Management, IT Governance, Risk Management, or Service Development. Domain-specific practices such as the TOGAF methodology for Enterprise Architecture, PMBOK or PRINCE2 for Project Management, and CMMI and SCRUM for Service Development can be used to complete the process model. In addition, there are numerous other standards and practices required to support specific controls, such as related to security management (ISO/IEC 27000 series) or risk management. These different practices and standards are typically defined at a high level, defining the requirements and activities to be performed within the IT organization. However, before they can be used in day-to-day practice they require a significant effort of design and detailing, often resulting in reinventing the wheel by each individual organization. As a result, the IT organization is challenged to create an overarching IT management model bringing it all together supported by an integrated IT management system.

So the challenge is to implement these practices into the actual workplace of an IT organization. Implementation requires the selection and implementation of IT management tools (or IT4IT tools) to support the different IT processes and activities. Typically, each software vendor has implemented their own interpretation of ITIL or other practices. While these standards say what needs to be done, additional guidance is needed to address how specific activities need to be performed and what data needs to be registered for each step. As a result, it is difficult to integrate solutions between multiple vendors (even with tools from the same vendor) and even more difficult to integrate and collaborate with external service providers.

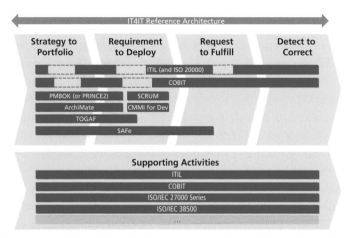

Figure 11: Positioning of ITIL and Other Key Practices Against the IT4IT Value Streams[1]

Typical challenges with these existing standards and best practices:

- Lacking full coverage of the entire service lifecycle; typically, multiple standards and practices need to be combined to provide a full management model. Standards are not "aligned"; each using their own terminology and data models.
- Lacking standard information (or data) models to enable data integration between IT management tools to increase transparency and improve decision-making.
- Focus on individual processes and activities but not defining consistent end-to-end workflows to deliver value to the business.
- No overarching model to melt the different best practices, frameworks, and standards into actual solutions that can be used to support day-to-day activities.
- Not prescriptive enough to guide how activities should be performed to enable automation and interoperability between IT management tools and service providers.

The last point is an important gap to discuss further. None of these frameworks provide a prescriptive model of how to actually perform IT management activities and what information models should be used. As a result, the actual implementation of ITIL varies a lot depending upon the specific tools used and

---

1   This figure does not display all IT management standards and best practices available in the market. Many additional standards and practices are defined for specific functions such as risk management, project portfolio management, security, and so on.

design decisions made by each IT organization. Tools from different vendors do not use the same terminology or data models even though they support ITIL processes. The outcome is that each IT organization and IT service provider has a substantially different way of working. Integration between IT management tools and external service providers is not trivial and becomes a burden due to lacking standards of how data is exchanged – and as a result coordination and collaboration between different teams is severely challenged. Information needed to monitor cost and performance of suppliers or to improve IT service delivery is not available and, as a result, the IT organization does not have the right controls in place to manage IT from a business perspective. This issue typically becomes apparent when dealing with outsourcing deals, where high costs are involved in aligning processes between vendors and building automated interfaces.

It is important to understand how interactions between the processes are executed – as well as the information (or data) that needs to be exchanged between systems and suppliers. Improving individual ITIL processes or specific IT tools such as a CMDB typically does not improve the end-to-end results of an IT organization. This leads to sub-optimization instead of supporting end-to-end value streams. The IT4IT approach provides a novel perspective – that the information model and the integrated systems (the IT management tools) should be the basis for managing IT.

The IT4IT value streams and IT4IT Reference Architecture provide the answer by defining an overall framework that can be used to identify the end-to-end workflows in the IT organization that create value of IT for the business. The IT4IT standard basically provides the bigger picture of managing IT services supporting the new IT operating model. This holistic picture is provided by the IT4IT value streams focusing on enabling end-to-end workflow instead of individual IT processes, practices, or methods.

To transition the IT organization to become the IT service broker and integrator, a reference model is needed to provide a framework of what is required to run this new IT environment. The IT organization needs to design, build, and implement a solid IT management capability that supports all IT processes through the lens of the IT4IT value streams. The IT4IT standard enables the implementation of this integrated IT management system (or IT4IT management system) to provide an optimized work environment for the IT employees as well as for the business to interact with the IT organization. This IT management system consists of all IT management tools, information, and interfaces to support all IT management activities; enabling fully automated workflows across the many different technologies, teams, and service providers.

The IT4IT approach is unique in that it provides a common information model with which to manage IT. In addition, it defines an overall architectural model supporting the selection and implementation of IT management software (solutions).

Improving how end-to-end processes are supported by information systems and can be automated is becoming a key differentiator for the IT service broker and orchestrator to demonstrate value to the business. Automation of IT management activities relies on a solid architecture of this IT management function, consisting of the value streams, IT processes, the required IT automation capabilities, required integrations, and data. The IT4IT Reference Architecture provides that foundation. The adoption of the IT4IT standard enables an IT organization to make consistent long-term investment decisions in IT management tools such as self-service portals, automated testing, deployment, and monitoring. This also enables the IT organization to interact consistently with its suppliers and – even more importantly – enables the IT function to gain deep and detailed insight into how well IT is performing and contributing to the business of which it is a part.

Figure 12 shows how the IT4IT standard should be used in combination with ITIL (and other practices).

At the top layer the IT4IT standard provides an integrated and holistic view using value streams. This layer is process and technology-agnostic. It provides the model of how the IT function should be working from an end-to-end perspective. The value streams can also be used as a governance model to assign ownership for IT management capabilities to support, evaluate, and continuously improve IT management practices. Every IT organization will benefit from the first step on the journey by adopting this holistic end-to-end view based upon the IT4IT value streams.

Next to that, a selective set of best practices needs to be chosen such as the TOGAF standard, ITIL, and PMBOK (or PRINCE2). These practices further

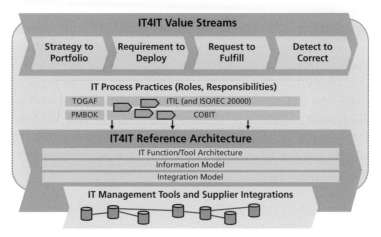

Figure 12: Using IT4IT to Provide Structure and the "Bigger Picture" for Managing IT

refine the requirements for specific areas such as project management, service development, and IT Service Management. The IT4IT Reference Architecture then provides the glue to incorporate these practices into an IT operating model that can be used to implement the entire IT function supported by automated tools and interfaces using a standard information model. ITIL can therefore still be used to define additional specifications for IT activities to be performed. COBIT can also be added to extend ITIL with specific controls and practices that can be audited and assessed from an IT governance perspective.

ITIL and the IT4IT standard are complementary. The IT4IT standard provides the bigger picture to integrate multiple practices needed to manage IT such as ITIL, SCRUM, and PMBOK. In addition, the IT4IT standard provides the architecture to define the target state IT operating model covering a prescriptive definition of how IT needs to work.

The IT4IT Reference Architecture is not based on greenfield thinking. IT4IT components can be added incrementally to existing practices to integrate, orchestrate, enhance, and enable the current way of working.

To run an IT organization you do not just want a process document (on paper); you want a working system. This means a real information system or solution that supports or automates these IT activities. All these activities within the value streams are in one way or another supported by IT management software products (tools). For this, a blueprint is needed defining all IT capabilities which can be automated or supported by IT tools. The IT4IT Reference Architecture is the perfect reference for this blueprint. It will be instrumental in defining a prescriptive model of how the activities within the value streams shall be supported by IT information systems. Next to that the IT4IT standard provides guidance of how the IT processes can be automated and information can be captured to support continuous improvement. This layer provides the IT4IT functional components, information model, and standard interfaces with suppliers.

Summarizing the relationship and unique proposition of the IT4IT Reference Architecture compared to existing frameworks and best practices:

- The IT4IT standard provides the overall end-to-end model of how the IT function should be managed using an IT Value Chain approach.
- The IT4IT standard helps to combine existing practices (such as ITIL) as well as emerging practices (such as SAFe) into a new IT operating model.
- The IT4IT standard provides new IT management practices such as DevOps, Agile, Lean software development, and Continuous Delivery.
- The IT4IT standard details how IT activities can be automated and supported by IT management tools (by defining a standard information model, functional components, and its interfaces).

Chapter 3

The IT4IT Standard in Detail

This chapter describes the IT Value Chain and IT4IT Reference Architecture in more detail. Together these provide the foundation for an IT operating model that can power a new style of IT, where the IT organization functions as a service broker to the lines of business.

Topics addressed in this chapter include:
- The IT Value Chain and value streams
- The IT4IT Reference Architecture

Chapter 4 describes the benefits and added value of using the IT4IT approach in more detail.

3.1 The IT Value Chain

A value chain is a series of activities that an organization performs in order to deliver something valuable, such as a product or service. Products pass through the activities of a chain in order and, at each activity, the product gains some value. A value chain helps organizations to identify the activities that are especially important for competitiveness – for the advancement of strategy and attainment of goals. The IT Value Chain is grouped into two main categories of activities:
- Primary activities, which are concerned with the production or delivery of goods or services for which a business function, like IT, is directly accountable.
- Supporting activities, which facilitate the efficiency and effectiveness of the primary activities.[2]

The IT4IT Reference Architecture identifies a number of key end-to-end workflows, referred to as value streams. These values streams define the integrated capabilities to manage IT from an end-to-end perspective.

---

[2] For more on the value chain concept, read Michael Porter's "Competitive Advantage: Creating and Sustaining Superior Performance".

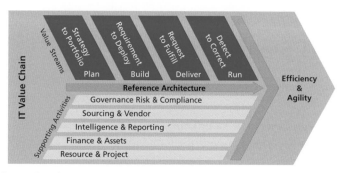

Figure 13: The IT Value Chain

The IT Value Chain content details the series of activities that every IT department performs that add value to a business service or IT service.

A key concept of the IT Value Chain is the IT service through which value is created to the business. Everything the IT organization is doing should be related to an IT service delivering value to the business, whether a person is working on a project, on a change, fulfilling service requests, or resolving incidents. Often this link to the IT service (or application) is not clearly defined and as a result the IT costs and added value of IT activities are not transparent and IT activities are not traceable. For example, a typical IT organization does not link projects to an IT service or application in their Project Portfolio Management (PPM) system. This type of linkage is, however, an essential element in managing the portfolio of investments and projects.

With services as the center of gravity, a value chain-based model for IT has been constructed by identifying the critical activities associated with the planning, sourcing, delivery, and management of services.

3.2   IT4IT Value Streams

The IT4IT standard breaks down the IT Value Chain into four (4) value streams to help IT consume the IT4IT Reference Architecture more easily. Each value stream represents a key area of value that IT provides across the full service lifecycle.

Each value stream is centered on a key aspect of the Service Model, the essential data objects (Information Model), and functional components (Functional

Model) that support it. Together, the four value streams play a vital role in helping IT control the Service Model as it advances through its lifecycle.

The four primary value streams are shown in Figure 14 and are as follows:
- Strategy to Portfolio (S2P)
- Requirement to Deploy (R2D)
- Request to Fulfill (R2F)
- Detect to Correct (D2C)

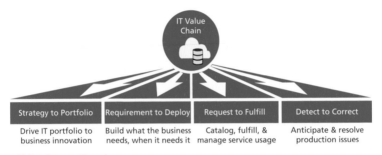

Strategy to Portfolio	Requirement to Deploy	Request to Fulfill	Detect to Correct
Drive IT portfolio to business innovation	Build what the business needs, when it needs it	Catalog, fulfill, & manage service usage	Anticipate & resolve production issues

Figure 14: Value Stream Overview

The primary value streams for the IT Value Chain generally align to what IT traditionally calls "Plan, Build, Deliver, Run". When used with an IT Value Chain-based model this is transformed into "Plan, Source, Offer, and Manage". These value streams are core to the IT function and have a vital role in helping to run the full service lifecycle holistically. These are usually hosted within IT.

The five supporting activities (as shown in Figure 7) for the IT Value Chain are:
- Governance Risk & Compliance
- Sourcing & Vendor
- Intelligence & Reporting
- Finance & Assets
- Resource & Project

The supporting activities help ensure the efficiency and effectiveness of the IT Value Chain and primary value streams. These can be corporate or administrative functions that are hosted in the lines of business and/or IT.

3.2.1   Strategy to Portfolio

The Strategy to Portfolio (S2P) Value Stream provides IT organizations with the optimal framework for interconnecting the different functions involved in managing the portfolio of services delivered to the enterprise to fulfill the organization's strategy. Activities such as capturing demand for IT services, prioritizing and forecasting investments, Enterprise Architecture, Service Portfolio Management, and Project Management require data consistency and transparency in order to maintain alignment between the business strategy and the IT portfolio.

 Strategy to Portfolio: Invest in the right services and align your IT portfolio with business strategy to make sound investments.

Typical questions to be answered within this value stream are:
- What IT services (and application) do I have within my portfolio?
- How well are these IT services aligned with the business strategy and business expectations (current and future demands)?
- What is the added value (and benefits) of the delivered IT services for the business?
- How much do these IT services cost? What are the risks?
- How can we simplify and rationalize the service portfolio?
- What standard technologies and infrastructure services are approved for use?
- How will IT services and technologies be sourced from different vendors?
- What investments in IT are needed? What projects must be initiated (or stopped)?
- What technologies are end-of-life and should be replaced or upgraded?
- How well did projects deliver their expected business benefits?
- How can I optimize the benefits and added value of the IT service portfolio?
- How does the roadmap look in the coming years? What are the key investment themes?

Traditional IT planning and Portfolio Management activities put emphasis on capturing and tracking a collection of *projects* that represent the "orders" from the business for technology enablement. The S2P Value Stream places emphasis on managing the portfolio of *services* and aims to provide a more holistic view of the IT portfolio to shape business investment decisions and connect IT costs with business value. It is not about the project, but rather about the outcome of a project being the IT service that delivers the benefits for the business. The IT services in the portfolio need to be continuously assessed to determine required improvements and to outline a long-term roadmap. Investments need to be line with these portfolio and service roadmaps to ensure the right investments are made. This requires that all demand, projects, and initiatives are linked to the IT service (or application) within the portfolio.

The key value propositions for adopting the S2P Value Stream are as follows:
- Establish a holistic IT portfolio view across the IT PMO, and the Enterprise Architecture and Service Portfolio functional components, so that IT portfolio decisions are based on business priorities.
- Use a well-defined system of record between the key areas that contribute to the IT Portfolio Management function to support consistent data for accurate visibility into business and IT demand.
- Endorse a Service Model that provides full service lifecycle tracking through conceptual, logical, and physical domains so it is possible to trace whether what was requested actually got delivered.

The key activities are:

Figure 15: Strategy to Portfolio Activities

The end-to-end IT portfolio view provided by the S2P Value Stream is accomplished by focusing on the service as the desired business outcome and exposing key data objects often unavailable using traditional planning methods. Defining the key data objects, the relationships between them, and their effect on the Service Model is core to the value stream approach. In addition, it provides inter-dependent functions such as Portfolio Demand, Enterprise Architecture, Service Portfolio, and Proposal functional components with data consistency and predefined data object exchanges in order to optimize the organization's IT Portfolio Management and service lifecycle management capability.

3.2.2 Requirement to Deploy

The Requirement to Deploy (R2D) Value Stream provides the framework for creating/sourcing new services or modifying those that already exist. The goal of this value stream is to ensure predictable, cost-effective, high quality results. It promotes high levels of re-use and the flexibility to support multi-sourcing. The R2D Value Stream is process-agnostic in that, while methods and processes may change, the functional components and data objects that comprise the value stream remain constant. Therefore, it is complementary to both traditional and new methods of service development like Agile, SCRUM, and DevOps.

 Requirement to Deploy: Define, build, test, and deploy new IT capabilities, at the right time, at the right cost (and with the right quality).

The R2D Value Stream consumes the Conceptual Service Blueprint produced in the S2P Value Stream and, through a series of design, development, and testing functions, produces data objects that represent the Logical Service Model for the service. The Logical Service Model is elaborated on until it represents a release that can be commissioned into a production state using standard deployment methods or in an on-demand manner using a user-driven catalog experience. Once deployed into a production state, the Physical Service Model is generated that comprises the physical elements of the service.

The R2D Value Stream ensures the service is developed to meet both the business requirements as well as the operations requirements (such as security, availability, maintainability, and performance). The R2D Value Stream is used both for custom developed applications as well as standard package based solutions, including:

- Custom developed applications (such as Java and .NET)
- Packaged based applications (such as CRM or ERP system)
- SaaS delivered applications (that also need some configuration changes such as configuring business rules, workflows, and interfaces)
- Infrastructure services (such as standard end-user computing services, hosting services)

This value stream manages all changes to the service (or application) during the entire lifecycle; whether it is a major release, minor release, or fixes for defects (or problems) found in production. Different development methods are supported such as Waterfall and Agile.

The key value propositions for adopting the R2D Value Stream are:
- Ensure that the Service Release meets business expectations (quality, utility).
- Make service delivery predictable, even across globally dispersed teams and suppliers, and multiple development methodologies, while preserving innovation.
- Standardize service development and delivery to the point where re-use of service components is the norm.
- Build a culture of collaboration between IT operations and development to improve Service Release success.

The key activities are:

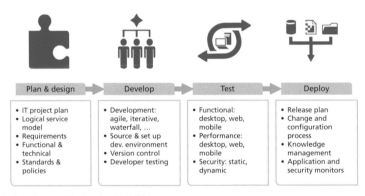

Plan & design	Develop	Test	Deploy
• IT project plan • Logical service model • Requirements • Functional & technical • Standards & policies	• Development: agile, iterative, waterfall, … • Source & set up dev. environment • Version control • Developer testing	• Functional: desktop, web, mobile • Performance: desktop, web, mobile • Security: static, dynamic	• Release plan • Change and configuration process • Knowledge management • Application and security monitors

Figure 16: Requirement to Deploy Activities

3.2.3   Request to Fulfill
The Request to Fulfill (R2F) Value Stream is a framework connecting the various consumers (business users, IT practitioners, or end customers) with goods and services that they need in order to drive productivity and innovation. This value stream places emphasis on time-to-value, repeatability, and consistency for consumers looking to request and obtain services from IT. It helps IT optimize both service consumption and fulfillment experiences for users by delineating functions for an Offer Catalog and Catalog Composition. The R2F Value Stream framework provides a single consumption experience to consumers for seamless subscription to both internal and external services, as well as managing

subscriptions and routing fulfillments to different service providers using the R2F Value Stream framework.

> Request to Fulfill: Source and provision quality services, enabling seamless consumption and usage monitoring.

This value stream ensures all services are orderable using a standard service catalog and self-service portal. It covers all activities from a request to the actual fulfillment of the request.

The R2F Value Stream plays an important role in helping IT organizations transition to a service broker model. Enterprise customers have been using external suppliers for goods and services for many years. The IT multi-sourcing environment will accelerate as companies adopt cloud computing offerings like Infrastructure as a Service (IaaS), Platform as a Service (PaaS), and Software as a Service (SaaS).

The key value propositions for adopting the R2F Value Stream are:
- Provide a portal and catalog blueprint for facilitating a service consumption experience that allows consumers to easily find and subscribe to services through self-service, regardless of sourcing approach.
- Establish the model for moving from traditional IT request management to service brokerage.
- Increase fulfillment efficiency through standard change deployment and automation.
- Leverage the common Service Model to reduce custom service request fulfillments and design automated fulfillments.
- Facilitate a holistic view and traceability across service Subscription, Usage, and chargeback.
- Improve the control on access to IT services and IT resources (as well as the auditability and compliance).
- Lower IT costs due to increased consumption control and improved utilization of IT resources (and licenses).

The key activities are:

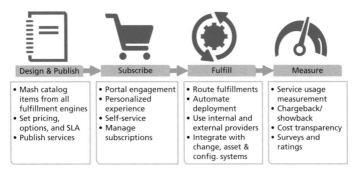

Figure 17: Request to Fulfill Activities

3.2.4 Detect to Correct

The Detect to Correct (D2C) Value Stream provides a framework for integrating the monitoring, management, remediation, and other operational aspects associated with realized services and/or those under construction. It also provides a comprehensive overview of the business of IT operations and the services these teams deliver. Anchored by the Service Model, the D2C Value Stream delivers new levels of insight, which help improve understanding of the inter-dependencies among the various operational domains; including event, incident, problem, change control, and configuration management. It also provides the business context for operational requests and new requirements. The D2C Value Stream is designed to accommodate a variety of sourcing methodologies across services, technologies, and functions. This value stream understands the inter-relationships and inter-dependencies required to fix operational issues. It supports IT business objectives of greater agility, improved uptime, and lower cost per service.

> Detect to Correct: Anticipate and resolve business execution issues, enhance results and efficiency. Create a feedback loop to go back to your portfolio and invest in the right services.

This value stream ensures continuous operation of IT services to the business. It continuously monitors the IT service and takes appropriate actions to ensure the system is available and performs as agreed. This includes activities from resolving incidents, tuning and assigning IT resources to optimize utilization and performance, mitigating security issues, proactive problem management, and providing end-user support to performing necessary housekeeping activities.

The D2C Value Stream provides a framework for bringing IT service operations functions together to enhance IT results and efficiencies. Data in each operation's domain is generally not shared with other domains because they do not understand which key data objects to share and do not have a common language for sharing. When projects are created to solve this, it is often too difficult and cumbersome to finish or there is an internal technology or organization shift that invalidates the result.

The D2C Value Stream defines the functional components and the data that needs to flow between components that enhance a business and service-oriented approach to maintenance, and facilitates dataflow to the other value streams.

The key value propositions for adopting the D2C Value Stream are:
- Prevent disruptions to business operations (caused by IT).
- Timely identification and prioritization of an issue.
- Improved data sharing to accelerate ability to understand the business impact.
- Automation, both within domains and across domains.
- Ensuring an operating model, capabilities, and processes that can handle the complexity of service delivery across multiple internal and external domains.
- Optimize IT resources assigned to or used by IT services (reduce over-capacity).
- Measure customer experience of using IT services.
- Effective linkage of events to incidents to problems to defects in the R2D Value Stream.

The key activities are:

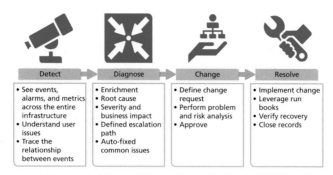

Figure 18: Detect to Correct Activities

3.3   The IT4IT Reference Architecture

The IT4IT Reference Architecture supports the IT Value Chain. It provides a prescriptive framework to support the value chain-based IT operating model and service-centric management ecosystem. It can be thought of as describing the "IT for IT" (IT4IT) architecture and relationships.

Previous methods for creating an IT4IT Reference Architecture in the IT management domain have been oriented around processes, capabilities, and technology implementations. Unfortunately, processes can be implemented differently for each IT organizational archetype, and capabilities are largely influenced by technology implementations. As a result, this architecture approach often results in a complex mesh of products and solutions requiring countless point-to-point integrations to accommodate the variations in process.

Instead, the IT4IT Reference Architecture approach for the IT Value Chain is anchored by four pillars – the Service Model, the Information Model, the Functional Model, and the Integration Model. These areas, when captured and modeled correctly, remain constant regardless of changes to process, technology, and/or capabilities.

The IT4IT Standard provides an Information Model

It is important to understand that the IT4IT standard is not a process model; it is complementary to process models. It defines how the IT Value Chain can be supported by information systems using a standard information model.

The IT4IT standard is neutral with respect to development and delivery models. It is designed to support Agile as well as Waterfall approaches, and Lean Kanban process approaches, as well as fully elaborated IT service management process models.

The IT4IT Reference Architecture is communicated using multiple levels of abstraction. Each abstraction level expands on the previous abstraction level to expose more details and prescriptive guidance. There are five levels. The upper levels (1-3) are vendor and technology-agnostic and provide more generic views that are suitable for strategy and planning purposes, as well as for creating IT management product roadmaps. The lower levels (4-5) provide more specific details, ultimately arriving at implementation level or vendor-owned/controlled information.

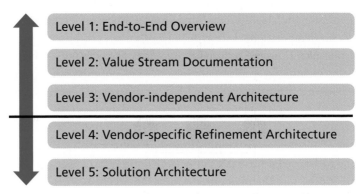

Figure 19: IT4IT Reference Architecture Levels

The IT4IT standard defines Levels 1 to 3. Levels 4 and 5 are not defined by the standard, which provides example guidance only at these levels. IT management software vendors, technology vendors, and IT service providers implement Levels 4 and 5.

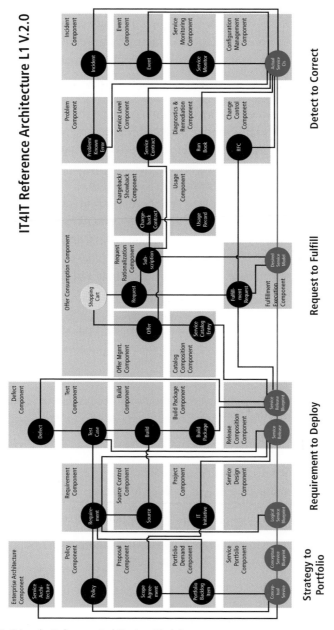

Figure 20: IT4IT Level 1 Reference Architecture Model

Figure 20 depicts the Level 1 model for the IT4IT Reference Architecture rendered using the informal notation. In discussions on the IT4IT Reference Architecture this graphic should be used to represent the content contained in abstraction Level 1.

The Level 1 architecture illustrates the focus on the entire IT Value Chain; everything from portfolio planning, design, development, and testing to training, deployment, data centers, help desk, and operations that keep everything running. The diagram contains the most important functional components to be implemented within the IT function. A functional component is a software building block or logical system supporting (or automating) IT management activities. IT represents the smallest unit of technology in the IT4IT Reference Architecture that can stand on its own and be useful as a whole to an IT practitioner (or IT service provider). Functional components manage specific IT management data and have defined inputs and outputs that are data objects.

A functional component is basically a logical system that needs to be present in any IT organization to provide specific management capabilities to support IT staff executing IT management activities.

Implementing the IT4IT standard requires a careful selection of IT management tools that support the identified interfaces to enable end-to-end workflows across the value streams.

The IT4IT Reference Architecture basically provides a blueprint to select and implement the IT management tools needed to manage the entire IT function. It defines the required interfaces to support end-to-end value streams as well as the information (or data) needed to take the right decisions. This model enables the automation of end-to-end IT processes to streamline operations and reduce costs.

Chapter 4
The Benefits of Using the IT4IT Standard

This chapter describes in detail the value and benefits that the IT4IT standard brings to the IT organization and its business.

This chapter covers the following topics:
- Benefits that can be achieved by implementing the IT4IT value streams and applying the IT4IT Reference Architecture
- An overview of all benefits of using the IT4IT standard grouped by stakeholder

Chapter 2 highlighted the constant pressure that the IT function is under to reduce costs, become more innovative, and support the business in its struggle to retain competitiveness and deliver faster with higher quality services. The IT organization needs to reinvent itself and become a service broker and integrator of IT services sourced from many different cloud service providers. But to realize this new IT organization, it is vitally important to implement an IT management system (an IT4IT system), providing a unified framework of processes, data, and IT solutions needed to enable this new role. The new IT organization is also much more dependent on automated tools and end-to-end processes, with improved transparency and visibility by using a common information model.

To realize this vision, a new IT operating model is needed which describes how the IT function can be automated and supported. Chapter 3 provided a high-level overview of this new operating model consisting of value streams and the IT4IT Reference Architecture. The IT4IT standard provides a fundamentally different approach to manage IT services across the entire IT Value Chain enabling better, faster, and cheaper IT service delivery with reduced risk. This chapter describes in more detail the value and benefits of using the IT4IT standard.

4.1   Benefits of Each IT4IT Value Stream

This section describes in more detail the benefits that can be realized for each
identified value stream.

Figure 21 summarizes the benefits of the IT4IT Reference Architecture (the
IT4IT benefits map).

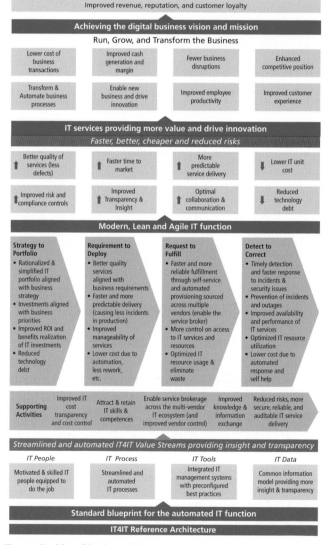

Figure 21: IT4IT as an Enabler of Business Value

As described in Chapter 2, the IT organization is facing a tremendous number of challenges. The IT organization needs to transform itself (or even reinvent itself) to ensure it can deliver on the expectations and demands of the business. A new IT operating model is needed to manage the new IT. The IT4IT Reference Architecture is an essential ingredient in enabling the transition to this new IT operating model, which address the following expectations:

- Optimize the value of IT delivered to the business; for example, supporting innovation and enabling new business models
- Transform and automate business processes
- Enhance customer experience
- Deliver business insight (by providing better information)
- Faster delivery of new or enhanced IT services aligned with business priorities
- Lower unit costs with more flexible sourcing and cost models to adapt to changing business demands
- Reduced risks through improved controls and transparency
- Faster response to potential security issues or other issues (minimizing the impact on the business)
- Better quality of services aligned with business requirements
- Improved transparency of IT
- Improved collaboration and communication between the business and IT

The IT organization becomes a service broker and integrator – creating hybrid environments – sourcing IT services from an increasing number of service providers; for example, hundreds of SaaS vendors and dozens of PaaS and IaaS vendors. As IT becomes more complex with this increasing number of vendors, IT management also becomes more dependent upon integrated end-to-end IT management solutions, which are delivered by an IT4IT organization. Such an integrated IT4IT solution consists of all functions, processes, tools, data, and integrations needed to manage the business of IT. While the current IT organization is heavily dependent upon manual activities performed by IT specialists, the new IT operating model is characterized by leveraging full automation of IT activities and self-service capabilities.

The business takes full control of the consumption and usage of IT services through an integrated IT service portal (or Engagement Experience Portal). The service portal provides the necessary insight in the value, cost, consumption, risks, and planned changes for the various services in the IT portfolio. In addition, the IT organization can automate end-to-end workflows organized around the IT4IT value streams. For example, using a continuous delivery pipeline to manage the end-to-end process from release planning, requirement collaboration (e.g., registered as user stories), support development activities, manage source codes, perform automated build, test to release in production – using automated tools.

The IT4IT Reference Architecture provides a unified framework and standard to enable the following strategic directions of the new IT organization:
- Manage IT as a business focusing on providing value to the business while controlling the costs, performance, and risks.
- Enable the IT function to become a Lean and Agile service provider sourcing, brokering, and orchestrating the delivery IT services (and infrastructure component services) across an increasing number of external service providers.
- Deliver and manage a more flexible and adaptable technology stack providing more elastic cost models based upon actual consumption (variable cost models which can be influenced by the business).
- Transition services and workload to the cloud; and subsequently manage large numbers of cloud vendors in an integrated and transparent manner.
- Adopt new IT management paradigms such as Lean, Agile, and Continuous Delivery. Use Continuous Delivery to deliver new releases much more quickly according to business requirements and with fewer defects (higher quality software at a high speed).
- Automate IT management tasks (such as build automation, test automation, deployment automation, but also robotic software to automatically respond to potential incidents or vulnerabilities) to improve productivity and reduce costs.
- Provide self-service and self-help capabilities (the user gains control).
- Improve the integration and collaboration across a more complex IT ecosystem with the growing number of external service providers and business partners.
- Leverage new technologies such as mobility, cloud, big data, Internet of Things (IoT), and Software-Defined Networking (SDN), but also leverage new delivery methods such as micro-services and containers for deployment.
- Enable the IT organization to continuously improve IT services through better visibility of metrics; for example, by having more insight in performance, cost, and capacity usage.

A key capability of the new IT organization is its ability to manage all IT service providers involved in the IT Value Chain (or ecosystem). Each vendor will implement and provide its own IT processes and IT management tools to deliver the services. This creates new challenges for the internal IT function to build and manage integrations with its vendors in the ecosystem to exchange data and integrate IT processes. The IT4IT Reference Architecture defines standard interfaces to collaborate and work seamlessly with all these external service providers.

4.1.1 Strategy to Portfolio

The primary focus of Strategy to Portfolio (S2P) is to manage a balanced IT service portfolio aligned with the business strategy and plans. Each IT service within the service portfolio needs to be managed throughout its lifecycle from an added value and investment perspective. The goal of the S2P Value Stream is to create an IT portfolio framework that allows IT organizations to optimize services provided to the business, by creating a holistic view of IT services, cost, value, risks, performance, and so on.

Traditionally, projects have been the focal point of IT governance and portfolio management processes. The shift, however, needs to be made by moving away from just monitoring and governing projects, towards monitoring the delivery and enhancement (and rationalization) of IT services. Benefits of investments are not realized by a project but through an operational IT service fulfilling the need of the business. IT investment decisions need to be focused on IT services, rather than individual projects. Thus, instead of prioritizing at the project level, a different approach is needed. First, all IT services are evaluated based on the business capabilities they support, the lifecycle phase, value, costs, architectural fit, risks, etc. Based upon this evaluation a roadmap is created and then resources (or budget) can be assigned against these prioritized IT services.

The S2P Value Stream defines a single funnel to manage all demands from the business and IT. All demands are managed through an integrated portfolio covering IT services (and applications), investments, and projects (or IT initiatives). The S2P Value Stream continuously evaluates the current portfolio and determines what needs to be improved, which investments and new developments are required, and so on. It consolidates the required changes into portfolio and service roadmaps aligned with changing business plans and goals.

Typical symptoms of deficiencies in the current S2P state of affairs in most IT organizations:

- Lacking a complete view of all IT services, applications, and technologies in the IT portfolio
- Lacking information and insight to identify rationalization opportunities and identify candidates for decommissioning
- Unplanned investments or projects to be executed (which could have been identified); for example, to perform necessary upgrades or mitigate risks (such as end-of-life)
- Complex and overlapping IT services and applications in the portfolio (room for rationalization and simplification)
- Poor data consistency and quality of the service portfolio administrations
- Inconsistent (or even undefined) service and IT portfolio management processes
- No single portfolio backlog to view all demands, ideas, improvement opportunities, and other proposed initiatives (no insight in all required and outstanding demands)
- IT does not understand business priorities
- Missing link between IT investments and business goals (and drivers)
- Investments and projects are not mapped to the IT services and applications in the portfolio; also the impact of projects on the run and maintain costs are not assessed
- Investment in non-strategic applications or applications that could (or should) have been decommissioned
- Lacking capabilities to prioritize IT investments (due to missing information to justify investments)
- The periodic budget cycle and investment planning is not transparent and traceable (often performed in spreadsheets)
- Long lead time to decommission applications (for example, due to unclear inter-dependencies and usage of the application)
- No insight in the complete funnel and in-flight initiatives (or projects)
- Lacking measurement of business benefits of investments and business value of IT services within the portfolio (no structured approach for IT benefits realization)
- IT is too slow and unresponsive to new demands and requirements
- IT projects fail or do not deliver the expected business value
- IT cannot communicate the performance, costs, risks, and added value of IT services

- IT projects not aligned with business plans and IT services (or application) roadmaps
- Slow IT budget cycles (typically yearly and not flexible)
- *Ad hoc* and unplanned initiatives (lacking a longer-term roadmap)
- Growing technology debt (for example, of outdated technologies or legacy applications to be upgraded)

The S2P Value Stream provides a blueprint for optimizing service and investment IT Portfolio Management. The S2P Value Stream allows the IT organization to better balance business demand, necessary technology refresh, regulatory, and other requirements with its budget and resource constraints. This value stream provides the following benefits:

- Consolidated view of the IT service, application, and technology portfolio (visibility and control of all IT services and related technologies)
- Ability to rationalize and simplify the IT service and application portfolio
- Accurate visibility of business and IT demand in an integrated portfolio backlog; having insight into the complete backlog covering demands, improvement opportunities, changes, required upgrades, or technology refresh initiatives
- Better alignment of IT strategy and service portfolio with business strategy and plans
- Balance the investment in innovation (change the business), enhancements, and technology refresh (run the business)
- Improved stewardship and control of IT Investments by linking investments in IT to business drivers and business benefits (and linking investments to IT services and applications in the portfolio)
- Improved understanding of the impact of investments on-the-run and maintain costs (of new or modified IT services affecting the yearly base cost of IT)
- Improved selection and prioritization of demands and projects (or IT initiatives) that provide the highest business value (IT investment portfolio management), as well as balancing the budget on innovation *versus* keeping the lights on
- More successful projects (or more likely that IT initiatives will realize its expected benefits)
- Standardized and simplified IT technology landscape (reduce complexity and diversity) by agreeing and defining technology standards

- Improved prioritization of demands for IT services aligned with business plans, regulatory requirements, technology policies, and IT roadmaps
- Optimize the value of the IT service portfolio and its investments considering IT budget constraints
- More business involvement in IT decisions (and helping the business to spot investment opportunities)
- Provide insight in performance, costs, risks, and added value of all IT services in the portfolio which improves decision-making and identifies portfolio rationalization opportunities
- Reduce technology debt (and risks) incurred with outdated technologies; for example, technologies that are end of support
- Reduced costs due to a rationalized and simplified IT landscape (and faster decommissioning of applications)
- Improved tracking of all (historic) investments in IT services (financial visibility)
- Improved tracking and realization of benefits of IT-related investments (improved IT benefits management); for example, by linking IT initiatives to IT services
- Prevent investments or IT spending (eliminate waste) in outdated or non-strategic applications (which should be decommissioned)
- Solid communication with (and involvement of) business stakeholders through IT roadmaps
- Timely cancellation of projects if they are not delivering the required outcome (or do not provide the expected value)
- Timely decommissioning (retirement) of IT services (or applications) not providing sufficient business value (continuously optimize the service portfolio)

Optimizing the IT service portfolio directly results in lower costs and improved alignment of IT services to business demand and business plans.

4.1.2   Requirement to Deploy

Requirement to Deploy (R2D) performs all activities to translate business requirements into design specifications and deliver high-quality IT services to the business. The design and development not only covers business requirements but also considers the development of all functionality needed to deploy, manage, and operate an application. This includes, for example, embedding monitoring capabilities such as standard logging, compliance to security, risk and identity management policies, performance, and daily operations tasks. This means building management-ready applications that can be monitored and efficiently managed throughout the lifecycle. Development needs to consider the entire lifecycle of an application (or service) to ensure the application can be properly managed.

The R2D Value Stream provides the following capabilities:
- Provide end-to-end traceability from requirement definition, development, build, test, to deployment
- Manage backlog of all work items such as requirements (or user stories), defects, development tasks, build and test tasks, and so on
- Collaborate with stakeholders related to requirements specification and design reviews
- Manage sprints and releases (integrated into the overall project and change calendar)
- Communicate progress and content or releases to stakeholders and users
- Manage source codes and builds in a consolidated repository
- Provide an integrated and automated delivery tool-chain for development, build, test, and deployment activities
- Provide security testing capabilities
- Perform load and performance testing
- Automatically update CMDB and license administration
- Integrate with investment and Project Portfolio Management (PPM)
- Integrate with automated deployment and provisioning; for example, to set up a temporary development and test environment
- Embed management capabilities into IT service and application (in the development phase), such as monitoring, housekeeping tasks, security and access management, and so on

This value stream provides the following benefits:
- Faster delivery of IT services due to Lean and Agile software development methods
- Faster delivery of fixes or patches to resolve production problems (or respond to security vulnerabilities)
- More successful releases of IT services to the business
- Improved visibility into the overall backlog of requirements, user stories, defects (or problems), etc. to be delivered

- Improved prioritization of selecting the requirements/user stories to be released first (based upon added value and business priorities)
- Make service delivery predictable, even across geographically dispersed teams, multiple suppliers, and multiple development methodologies
- Provide end-to-end traceability from requirement initiation to actual deployment
- Automation of IT tasks resulting in lower costs, faster delivery, and improved quality
- Reduced development and maintenance cost due to better control on customizations and configuration changes (for example, prevent building features that are not necessary or have a low business value)
- Better quality of software due to improved communication and collaboration with business and other stakeholders (and as a result higher customer satisfaction)
- Improved throughput of the continuous delivery factory (more requirements and user stories delivered)
- Ensure that each service release is high quality, fit-for-purpose, and meets customer expectations
- Build a culture of collaboration between the business, IT development, and IT operations (bridging the gaps)
- Increased management information for traceability and benchmarking of internal and external service developers and suppliers
- Increased re-use of service components (and functions) between projects (and applications)
- Improved productivity of IT developers and testers due to automation and improved access to integrated data (such as requirements linked to development tasks, source codes, test cases, defects, etc.)
- Reduced security risks by creating designs with security and compliance in mind
- Reduced number of defects in release causing operational issues (which results in lower cost of supporting applications due to a lower number of incidents)
- Reduced operations cost due to incorporating management capabilities during the development phase, such as monitoring (for example, using standard logging), performing daily operations tasks, resource scaling, and so on
- Improved information and insight in order to continuously improve development and test processes

- Increased visibility and control on external vendors involved in the development and testing of IT services
- Establish control points to manage the quality, utility, security, and cost of services independent of development methodology or technology
- Reduced development costs by preventing building software features not used or not providing value
- Improved predictability ensuring that the application or service delivered actually performs as requested, leading to higher rates of user acceptance and better business alignment
- Reduced risk of project failure by taking an iterative approach
- Improved communication with stakeholders of the planned releases (and its content)

The IT organization as a factory?

The IT organization is often seen as a factory, working on IT activities according to standard processes. People talk in terms of processes, plans, input and output, throughput, and performance. For example, think about the tool-chain defining an assembly line for Java or .NET applications going through different stations such as design, code, build, test, and deploy. However, we should not forget that IT services delivered by projects are different each time and it requires a lot of creativity to solve new challenges and problems. Knowledge workers are performing a large amount of this work. Empowerment is therefore needed to ensure the IT knowledge worker has the freedom to take the right decisions.

An IT organization needs to recruit skilled and experienced people. Today's environment is more complex than ever. IT management tools help but, in the end, people with the right skills and experience deliver the best results. An excellent project manager and architect or technical lead can help provide the ultimate success.

4.1.3   Request to Fulfill

The Request to Fulfill (R2F) Value Stream represents a modern, consumption-driven engagement model and goes beyond the traditional IT service request management. It is a framework for connecting the various consumers (business users, IT practitioners, or end customers) with goods and services that they need to drive productivity and innovation. It fosters service consumption and fulfillment, knowledge sharing, self-service support, and collaboration between communities of interest to improve the overall engagement experience with IT. The R2F Value Stream plays an important role in helping IT organizations advance toward a service broker model.

The IT organization manages a growing amount of recurring service requests, both from the business as well as initiated by IT staff or automated systems, for example:

- Standard end-user computing requests (e.g., new laptop, mobile devices, etc.) or requests for additional software
- Request new infrastructure resources (e.g., a new virtual machine, database, firewall rules, network changes, etc.)
- Modify capacity and resource allocation (e.g., CPU, memory, disk, etc.)
- Deploy new releases on a test or production environment
- Access requests (to business applications and other IT resources)
- Password resets
- HR and IT user account changes (joiner, mover, or leaver)
- Various requests such as to import data, create a report, and so on

These requests are today typically executed manually by various teams, each using different tools and procedures. Often the IT organization does not have a single catalog published through a standard web shop front-end, but rather has many different channels to request services (or even through unstructured emails). There is also a huge opportunity to automate the current manual request fulfillment activities to reduce cost and speed up the delivery.

The R2F Value Stream supports the end-to-end process from requesting a service from the catalog, through approvals, to the activation or provisioning of the service for the user. After activation of the service, the actual consumption and costs are monitored to provide showback (or chargeback) to the consumer. This is done to make the user aware of the costs and to influence the actual usage of the service. In addition, policies can be defined to automatically invoke a subscription (remove the access rights) or remove software; for example, if a user does not log in or use the service for a specific period of time.

This value stream covers capabilities such as:

- Define and publish a standard (and rationalized) service catalog consolidating and aggregating catalogs from different service providers and partners.

- Self-service portal (and catalog) to provide easy access to request or modify subscriptions of services.
- Support the entire workflow covering the necessary approvals, orchestration of fulfillment activities across different technologies and vendors, including monitoring against SLA and/or agreed delivery plans.
- Automate the activation or provisioning of services (for example, deploying software, modifying user access rights, and so on).
- Activate usage monitoring and provide feedback of resource usage and related costs; also challenge the end-user to retire subscriptions in cases where the service is not used (or rarely used).
- Automatically update the CMDB and subscription administration (of users subscribed to IT services) based upon executed service requests.
- Control access of users (and systems) to business applications and other IT resources; ensure all controls are in place to manage the approval and access to IT services.
- Manage subscriptions and access rights of users subscribed to IT services (or applications).
- Automatically deactivate subscriptions if the agreed contract period ends (for example, remove access rights of user to a business application).
- Understand actual usage of an IT services and related IT resources (capacity usage).
- Provide showback (or IT chargeback) to the business of IT services based upon actual resource consumption.
- Automated deployment of new IT service or application releases (triggered by the R2D Value Stream).

The R2F Value Stream places emphasis on time-to-value, repeatability, and consistency for consumers looking to request and obtain services from IT. It optimizes both service consumption and fulfillment experiences by delineating between the creation of offers and catalog aggregation and Service Catalog Entry composition.

Today IT organizations struggle to increase the ratio of self-sourced services over workflow-based fulfillment requiring direct human intervention. Many fulfillments today require too much intervention that consumes valuable IT resources. By increasing self-sourcing, companies will see improved business velocity and reduction in friction. They are also able to reduce "shadow-sourcing" within the lines of business because of a more responsive consumption experience. Today's IT is focused on delivery of technical capabilities – tomorrow's IT must be positioned to focus on facilitating consumption of multi-sourced services.

The R2F Value Stream provides the following benefits:

- Automation of repetitive/recurring IT activities related to the deployment and provisioning of IT services (including password resets, installation and configuration of software, deployment of new servers or databases, provision of access to IT resources, add/modify capacity allocation, etc.), resulting in lower costs and faster delivery with fewer failures or exceptions.
- Improve customer experience as a result of easy access to IT services through a self-service portal.
- Improve transparency of the progress and actual status of the fulfillment workflow (including approvals).
- Influence consumption and demand for IT services (due to showback of actual usage and costs, making end-users aware of costs associated with consumption).
- Optimize the usage of capacity and licenses (due to actively monitoring and providing feedback to the customer automatically).
- Provide traceability of all changes in the IT landscape; simplifying and improving auditing.
- Brokering and (automated) selection of the most appropriate IT service provider for fulfillment (e.g., IaaS cloud vendor) depending upon the request, company policies, resource needs, and actual tariff and pricing structure.
- Reduce the number of errors as a result of automated provisioning and deployment (compared to manual activities performed for the activation of a service).
- Reduce the number of IT staff needed to handle requests and provisioning due to automation and self-service capabilities (improved productivity of IT staff).
- Improve control over access rights of users to IT services, applications, and IT resources (part of IAM). Ability to audit actual access rights against the approved subscription administration.
- Improve control and auditability of all requests and related changes in the IT landscape (due to a standard request management system, approval workflows, and demand policies).
- Reduce the risks of unauthorized access to IT resources (and ensure compliance with security and risk policies such as segregation of duties).

- Reduce complexity of the IT landscape due to standardized service catalogs (and defined standard technologies to be used).
- Optimize capacity and license utilization; for example, actively down-scaling resources if not used to reduce waste. Enables increased cost optimization; for example, by canceling expired subscriptions and reclaiming resources, subscriptions, and/or licenses that are unused.
- Ability to actively move workloads, up-scale or down-scale (auto-scaling) depending upon usage patterns (triggered by the D2C Value Stream), resulting in lower IT costs and improved performance.
- Improve cost transparency of IT resources allocated and used to deliver IT services.
- Automatically update the CMDB and related service models based upon deployment activities (ensure that deployed infrastructure components are linked to the IT service or application).

Summarizing these benefits results in the following outcome for the IT function:
- Reduced cost to fulfill service requests (due to automated and improved productivity).
- Lower IT operations cost due to lower consumption (due to improved utilization of IT resources, active influence of demand, and eliminating waste or unused subscriptions), but also as a result of lower effort to maintain IT services due to the deployment of standard configurations and settings applied during provisioning.
- Faster delivery of requested services with fewer errors (resulting in less rework and incidents).
- Improved customer experience and satisfaction (due to better and faster delivery).
- Improved productivity of business and its users (due to faster delivery with fewer errors).
- Reduced risks of unauthorized or unwanted access of users to IT resources (improved access controls).

4.1.4 Detect to Correct

The Detect to Correct (D2C) Value Stream ensures continuous operations by supporting the end-to-end process of detecting (potential) exceptions and minimizing the impact on the business. The focus is on preventing incidents from occurring by taking proactive measures and timely detection of potential issues.

The scope of the D2C Value Stream includes all deviations related to policies, agreed schedules, agreements (and expectations), or SLA targets. For example:

- Detect and correct all potential disruptions or degradations of a service such as outages, performance issues, and security events (for example, vulnerabilities).
- Correct exceptions of configurations settings against security policies and configuration baselines (monitor configurations against defined target states and baselines).
- Monitor and act upon unauthorized usage of IT services or access to resources.
- Monitor and optimize IT resources assigned to IT services (based upon usage patterns and defined policies). For example, perform auto-scaling during peak hours or turn off assigned resources to reduce costs.
- Measure customer experience (and collect feedback).
- Detect and act upon authorized access to IT services, applications, and IT assets.
- Act upon security vulnerabilities and other security-related issues.
- Ensure production is executed according to planned and agreed schedules (for example, monitoring backup, job, and production schedules).

The D2C Value Stream covers capabilities such as:

- Proactively monitor IT services to detect potential issues before the customer or business is affected.
- Use data analytics tools to monitor logs and other machine data to understand trends and identify usage patterns.
- Collect, filter, and consolidate events and data from different monitoring tools.
- Consolidated event management system to filter and correlate events (identify events to be acted upon).
- Effective linkage of events and incidents to affected IT services used by the business (and understand the impact on the business process).
- Automatically respond to exceptions or events; for example, by initiating automated recovery actions and/or implementing workarounds.
- Conduct service impact assessment of detected exceptions and events to business services using the CMDB (and defined service models).
- Automatically create an incident and assign it to responsible teams (or external parties).
- Monitor progress of resolution against SLA targets.

- Provide capabilities to support root cause analysis.
- Maintain known errors and workarounds for recurring incidents.
- Manage and monitor daily operations tasks such as backup and job schedules.
- Automatically modify assigned IT resources (capacity) in case of changed usage patterns and workload (for example, auto-scaling).
- Provide self-help for end-users to find a solution in the knowledge base.
- Provide self-service for end-users through an IT service portal to raise new incidents or questions.
- Leverage social media, communication, and collaboration tools to improve interaction with the business and IT.
- Identity unauthorized access or unauthorized changes to IT services, applications, and other IT assets.
- Automatically inform business and other stakeholders of potential incidents and unplanned outages.
- Provide a knowledge base to record standard solutions, FAQ, and other guidelines.
- Initiate business and service continuity plans (if appropriate).
- Continuously improve monitoring capabilities in case occurred incidents were not detected by existing service monitors.
- Integration of ticketing with external IT service providers (to dispatch or receive incidents).
- Coordinate incident and problem resolution in a complex multi-vendor ecosystem (triage role).
- Conduct customer survey after reported incidents has been resolved.
- Integrate the identified problems into the product backlog (managed by development).

The benefits achieved with the IT4IT approach for the D2C Value Stream are:
- Timely identification of an issue before users of the service (or business services) are impacted, resulting in less down time, fewer business disruptions, and improved customer satisfaction.
- Improved prioritization of issues (detected events, security issues, end-user reported incidents, etc.) based upon the impact to the business.
- Fewer unplanned/*ad hoc* activities or emergency changes.
- Faster resolution of incidents (from detection to correction); reducing the impact of incidents to the business.
- Reduced support costs by providing self-service and self-help capabilities to the user community (less need to call the service desk).

- Reduced number of incidents due to better quality of IT services.
- Prevention of incidents (and outages) due to proactive monitoring and proactive problem management.
- More time available for prevention and to improve operations (less fire-fighting and rework activities).
- Automated resolution of events/incidents using automation tools (less human intervention needed).
- Improved utilization of IT resources due to capacity monitoring and tuning (using standard policies).
- Insight into customer experience of using IT services.
- Improved communication and collaboration with stakeholders and users (for example, publish outages to a portal).
- Improved customer experience and satisfaction (for example, due to reduced business disruptions, better communication, self-help, and so on).
- Reduced effort and time needed to diagnose incidents and problems to identify the root cause; and/or identify the responsible team or vendor to resolve the issue.
- Improved availability and performance of IT services (due to continuous measurement; evaluation; improving the monitoring function).
- Improved handover from development to support (resulting in better alignment; faster resolution of incidents).
- Improved control and integration with external service providers (for example, to dispatch incidents); resulting in reduced cost for coordinating end-to-end service delivery across multiple vendors.
- Improved feedback to development teams to enable the continuous improvement of IT services; for example, by sharing problems identified in production with development (creating an integrated backlog of problems, new features, and so on).

4.1.5   Supporting Activities

4.1.5.1   *Governance, Risk, and Compliance*

This supporting process manages the overall Governance, Risk, and Compliance (GRC) activities. This includes, for example:

- Define controls and control practices (for example, for security, compliance, IAM, suppliers).
- Define and publish policies related to IT GRC.
- Perform risk assessments such as Business Impact Assessments (BIA).

- Perform periodic audits.
- Manage audit findings and identify improvement opportunities.
- Manage risks and compliance of IT services and related infrastructure.

The benefits of using the IT4IT Reference Architecture for this supporting activity include:
- Reduced exposure to risks and penalties.
- Lower cost of managing audits, controls, and compliance (due to improved integration and transparency).
- IT risk information available for all IT activities (such as during service portfolio assessments).
- Improved control and transparency of risks and compliance issues related to IT service delivery.
- Ability to monitor and report compliance.

4.1.5.2 Sourcing and Vendor

This supporting process manages the vendors and partners involved in the IT service value chain such as technology vendors and IT service providers. This includes, for example:
- Perform sourcing activities (such as negotiation with vendors).
- Manage vendor/supplier information.
- Monitor and report vendor performance.
- Manage vendor escalations and exceptions.
- Actively manage contracts with the vendors (and contract reviews).

The benefits of using the IT4IT Reference Architecture for this supporting activity include:
- Reduced cost for managing contracts and vendors due to better information and transparency (easier to understand performance of suppliers).
- Improved contract utilization and timely modification and cancellation.
- Improved collaboration and communication with vendors; more flexible partnerships due to open interfaces.
- Improved selection and sourcing of IT service providers within the IT Value Chain.
- Improved transparency and visibility of the performance of IT service providers involved in the IT ecosystem.
- Standardized methods of managing contracts with the growing number of vendors in the IT ecosystem.

4.1.5.3 Intelligence and Reporting

This supporting process provides the capabilities related to business intelligence, reports, scorecards, and dashboards. This includes, for example:

- Define key metrics and KPIs to manage the business of IT.
- Provide self-service reporting and data analytics.
- Provide easy access to consolidated IT management information.
- Publish standard metrics and KPIs to support continuous improvement.
- Provide standard reporting for all IT processes.

The benefits of using the IT4IT Reference Architecture for this supporting activity include:

- Lower cost of creating IT service reports and monitoring key metrics.
- Improved productivity of IT employees and business users searching for information (easy access to IT data).
- More accurate and timely access to information across different IT management data sources.
- Improved decision-making due to better information (common data model) to support continuous information.
- Ability to provide an integrated view on IT management data managed by different vendors, tools, or teams.

4.1.5.4 Finance and Assets

This supporting process provides the financial management capabilities for managing IT financials. This includes, for example:

- Manage IT budgets.
- Manage all IT costs (such as HR costs, contracts and licenses, hosting and other subscription costs, managed services contracts).
- Define consumption-based IT cost model (using the IT service model).
- Calculate IT costs per service; determine tariff and pricing models.
- Perform charging and showback.
- Cost forecasting.
- Perform benchmarking.
- Match and validate invoices from vendors to the actual service delivery (for example, applications and infrastructure components defined in the CMDB).
- Manage accounts payable and invoices of vendors (including invoice verification).

The benefits of using the IT4IT Reference Architecture for this supporting activity include:

- Improved cost transparency of IT services (using a consumption-based model) to the business and end-users.
- Ability to influence and reduce costs (by the business).
- Understand cost impact of new changes and projects (on-the-run and maintain costs).
- Improved invoice verification of consumption and costs related to the CMDB, request management system, and contract management system.
- Improved investment decision-making due to better insight in actual costs and potential impact upon run-and-maintain of proposed changes.

4.1.5.5 Resource and Project

This supporting activity ensures the right skills and competences are available to transition the IT organization to a service broker and integrator. This activity covers talent management but also requires attracting, developing, and retaining IT personnel. This support activity is closely related to the overall HR function within the company.

Key activities:
- Manage IT skills and competences.
- Plan, source, and execute training (and education).
- Perform resource planning (IT employees) for project resources as well as operations activities.
- Acquire and retain HR resources.
- Alignment with overall enterprise HR function.
- Build relationships with external parties to deliver HR capabilities.

Typically, issues with these current HR supporting activities are:
- Lacking insight in actual performance of IT staff (managers are not really aware what IT specialists are doing).
- Limited growth and career opportunities.
- Innovative and "nice" projects are given to external, temporary staff.
- Dependency upon a few skilled IT people (which need to be involved in all projects and major issues).

The benefits of using the IT4IT Reference Architecture for this supporting activity include:

- Optimal match between skilled resources and actual demand.
- Improved employee satisfaction due to career planning and continuous learning (providing the training and practices to do their job).
- A motivated and skilled resource pool.
- Ability to source IT staff at the right time.
- Ability to develop and retain scarce IT skills and competences.
- Optimized utilization of scarce IT employee resources.
- Building the required culture for the new IT organization.

4.2   Benefits per Stakeholder

This section provides a brief overview of the benefits grouped by stakeholder. The benefits of the IT4IT standard can be cascaded from having an integrated IT4IT capability for the IT function up to the benefits for the business (and its customers). Having a solid IT4IT system results in better performance of the IT function as a whole. Smoothly operated IT results in more aligned and better service delivery to the business; the business is enabled to improve its competitive position in the market and satisfy customers.

The benefits of having an IT4IT standard can be related to the different parties involved:

- Business (and customers); benefits for the business by having a smoothly operated IT function.
- IT function or organization; benefits for the IT organization and its IT employees for having good IT management tools, data, and processes to support their work.
- IT4IT organization; benefits for the teams that are developing and managing the IT management tools.
- IT service providers; benefits for the IT service providers involved in the IT ecosystem.
- IT tool vendors; benefits of adopting the IT4IT standard for vendors involved in the delivery of standard IT management solutions.

The following sections provide an overview of the key benefits per target audience. Per stakeholder, the specific benefits are identified.

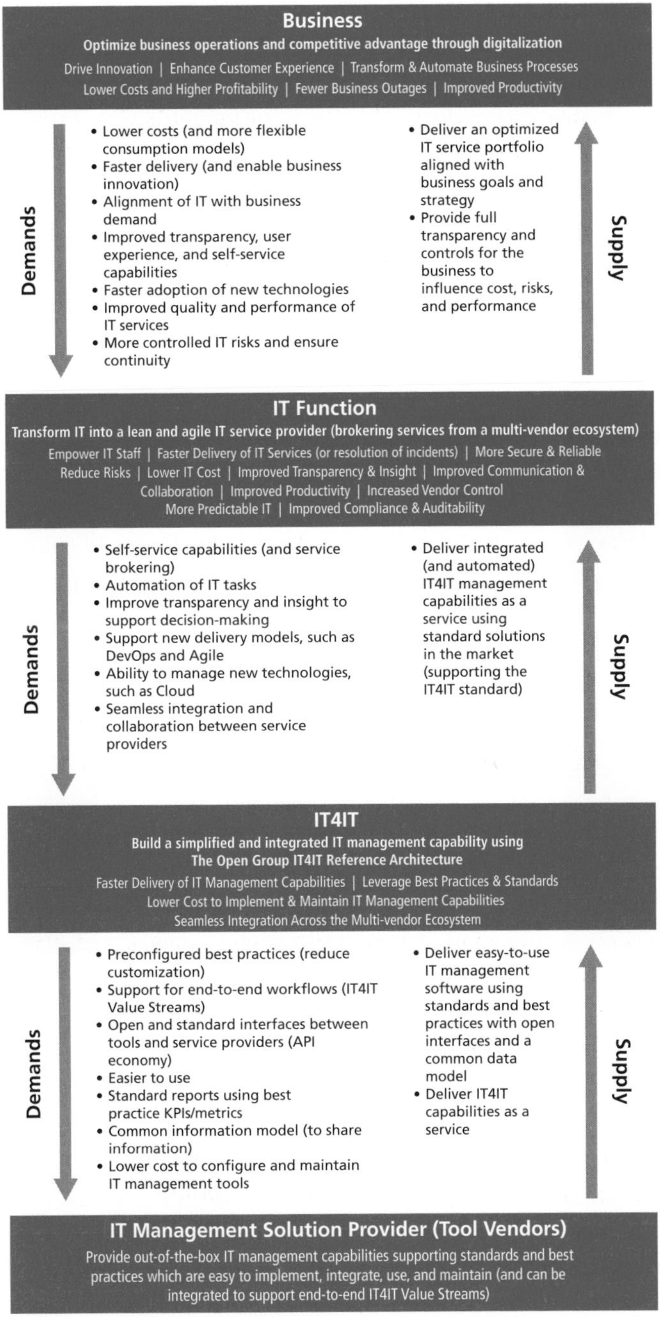

Business

Optimize business operations and competitive advantage through digitalization

Drive Innovation | Enhance Customer Experience | Transform & Automate Business Processes
Lower Costs and Higher Profitability | Fewer Business Outages | Improved Productivity

Demands

- Lower costs (and more flexible consumption models)
- Faster delivery (and enable business innovation)
- Alignment of IT with business demand
- Improved transparency, user experience, and self-service capabilities
- Faster adoption of new technologies
- Improved quality and performance of IT services
- More controlled IT risks and ensure continuity

Supply

- Deliver an optimized IT service portfolio aligned with business goals and strategy
- Provide full transparency and controls for the business to influence cost, risks, and performance

IT Function

Transform IT into a lean and agile IT service provider (brokering services from a multi-vendor ecosystem)

Empower IT Staff | Faster Delivery of IT Services (or resolution of incidents) | More Secure & Reliable
Reduce Risks | Lower IT Cost | Improved Transparency & Insight | Improved Communication &
Collaboration | Improved Productivity | Increased Vendor Control
More Predictable IT | Improved Compliance & Auditability

Demands

- Self-service capabilities (and service brokering)
- Automation of IT tasks
- Improve transparency and insight to support decision-making
- Support new delivery models, such as DevOps and Agile
- Ability to manage new technologies, such as Cloud
- Seamless integration and collaboration between service providers

Supply

- Deliver integrated (and automated) IT4IT management capabilities as a service using standard solutions in the market (supporting the IT4IT standard)

IT4IT

**Build a simplified and integrated IT management capability using
The Open Group IT4IT Reference Architecture**

Faster Delivery of IT Management Capabilities | Leverage Best Practices & Standards
Lower Cost to Implement & Maintain IT Management Capabilities
Seamless Integration Across the Multi-vendor Ecosystem

Demands

- Preconfigured best practices (reduce customization)
- Support for end-to-end workflows (IT4IT Value Streams)
- Open and standard interfaces between tools and service providers (API economy)
- Easier to use
- Standard reports using best practice KPIs/metrics
- Common information model (to share information)
- Lower cost to configure and maintain IT management tools

Supply

- Deliver easy-to-use IT management software using standards and best practices with open interfaces and a common data model
- Deliver IT4IT capabilities as a service

IT Management Solution Provider (Tool Vendors)

Provide out-of-the-box IT management capabilities supporting standards and best
practices which are easy to implement, integrate, use, and maintain (and can be
integrated to support end-to-end IT4IT Value Streams)

Figure 22: Stakeholder Benefits Map

4.2.1 Business (and IT Users)

IT is an enabler of business differentiation and improving customer experience. A well-functioning IT organization improves the competitive position of the business, enables cost reduction, improves productivity, and streamlines business processes. IT enables optimum communication between business, customers, and business partners. This is achieved by creating a portfolio of IT services aligned with business objectives. These IT services need to be designed, developed, deployed, and continuously operated. The IT4IT approach is the enabler for the IT organization to ensure these IT services can be effectively and efficiently delivered to the business.

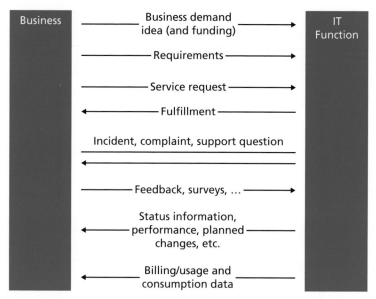

Figure 23: Examples of Interactions between Business and IT

The benefits for the business have been described in the previous sections grouped by IT4IT value stream. This section describes the benefits of the business specifically related to using the IT4IT solutions interacting with the business. The business uses the IT services provided by the IT organization such as end-user computing services, ERP system, CRM system, email, document management, business intelligence, and so on. But the business is also using IT4IT services to directly interact with the IT organization such as:

- Demand portal to raise new demands, ideas, or requirements (opportunity funnel).

- Self-service portal to browse the IT service catalog and request IT services (for example, access requests to business applications, request new laptop or mobile phone).
- View actual status of IT services and planned changes (or releases).
- Self-help to resolve incidents, find relevant documentation and user guides, find answers to frequently asked questions (using a knowledge base), or register a new incident or complaint.
- Consumption portal to view subscriptions to IT services including actual consumption and cost information (with the option to modify or unsubscribe to services).
- Easy access to documentation and user guides (such as end-user guides).
- Participate in design reviews and user acceptance tests (to collaborate with the development teams).
- Customer survey tool to participate in service reviews and provide feedback to the IT organization (enabling continuous feedback).
- Participate in service reviews and involvement in defining roadmaps and prioritizing business demands.
- Access management service to allow users easy access to all applications and services (and support password resets or single sign-on).

IT4IT solutions basically improve communication and collaboration between the business and IT, resulting in more transparency, but also ensuring the business is in control of the IT consumption (and influencing the costs). An IT4IT solution provides a consolidated service portal – the Engagement Experience Portal – for the user to view all relevant IT management information in their own individual context. These IT4IT services delivered to the business enable the consumer to control the consumption and cost of IT services. It provides the required transparency of the performance, cost, value, and risks of IT services for the business. It optimizes the communication and collaboration with the business; for example, by publishing major incidents, emergency changes, or any other planned change in the release schedule. With the implementation of an integrated IT service portal a user can more easily communicate and collaborate with the IT organization. Using a self-service portal, an end-user can request services from the service catalog, browse through a knowledge base to find solutions, find documents and user guides, raise incidents, and so on.

Having these IT4IT capabilities delivered to the business users provides a number of benefits for the business (as owners and consumers of IT services):

- Cost transparency; understand the consumption and cost of IT services and provide the ability to directly influence costs through available choices (business in the driver seat).
- Improved productivity due to faster and better resolution of incidents and questions (for example, using self-help).
- Improved alignment and prioritizing of demands and investments due to better collaboration with IT.
- Improved capturing and discussion of requirements with the IT organization (resulting in better services aligned to business needs).
- Improved communication and collaboration between business and IT resulting in better user experience and customer satisfaction.
- Improved user experience and higher customer satisfaction (due to optimized communication and collaboration with the IT function).
- Ability to receive services cheaper and faster through self-service (faster fulfillment of service requests; for example, request access to a business application).
- Ability to influence and manage IT consumption and costs (business is in control).
- Improved productivity by providing easier access to IT services via a standard service catalog and portal (single point of contact).

4.2.2 The IT Organization

The IT4IT standard provides the framework to support all activities performed by IT knowledge workers within the IT organization. The IT4IT Reference Architecture enables the internal IT department to transform itself to become a Lean and Agile service broker and integrator. It provides the capability to manage a hybrid IT environment of both internal IT as well as managing the multi-vendor cloud ecosystem – enabling full control to determine the most appropriate sourcing models.

The IT4IT approach enables the support and automation of end-to-end processes across different applications, technology platforms, and service providers. The need for solid integration and fluid workflows is becoming more important for the new IT function. For example, the activities involved in the end-to-end workflow from detecting an incident through resolution covers a broad range of activities supported by different tools and administrations, as illustrated in Table 3.

Table 3: Example Tools and Administrations for the Detect to Correct Value Stream

Examples of Activities Involved in the Detect to Correct (D2C) Value Stream	Examples of Tools and Administrations to Support these Activities or Provide the Necessary Information
• Services are monitored and an exception or event is raised. • The event is correlated against other relevant events and data collected. • The service impact to the business is determined (using the service model from the CMDB). • An incident is created and assigned to responsible team (and potentially matched to reporting incidents by users). • If available, use automated recovery procedures or run books to restore the service. • Stakeholders are automatically notified and kept informed of the progress (using the subscription administration). • Recent changes in the IT landscape are reviewed that could have caused the incident. • The knowledge base is checked for known errors. • The incident is further analyzed and diagnosed. • Support collaboration and communication with different teams and vendors (if needed). • Root cause analysis is performed. • Potentially dispatch incident to third parties to support the analysis and resolution. • Meanwhile monitor incident resolution against SLA targets and keep stakeholders informed. • Solution or workaround is identified (and documented). • Solution (or fix) is implemented. • Solution is verified (and customer is informed). • Incident and event is closed. • Conduct after action review (and capture learning). • Perform customer survey (or incident review).	• Monitoring tools (such as security monitoring, synthetic transactions, application performance monitoring, system monitoring, etc.) • Operations data analytic tools (such as collecting machine data and logs) • Event management system (to correlate and filter events) • CMDB (providing the actual deployed service model) • Incident management system • Change management system • Chat and/or email system (and other collaboration and communication tools) • Knowledge base • Diagnostic tools • Operations and element manager tools (tools used to manage specific technologies such as storage, hardware, network, system, or database management tools) • IT automation and run book tools • Deployment tools, provisioning tools, and tools to configure systems (e.g., install patch, restart a service, modify capacity, etc.)

As shown in the table, there are many activities involved in the workflow from detection to correction, which are performed by different teams (and vendors) using multiple tools and many data sources. The IT4IT Reference Architecture provides the ability to integrate and standardize these activities across the value stream including the ability to support collaboration and sharing of information.

Without integration of these systems, resolving incidents takes more time and effort. Currently the IT organization is dependent upon a large amount of human intervention and manually performed analysis and recovery actions. Without an IT4IT standard the possibility of automating recovery actions becomes challenging. A complicating factor is the increasing number of vendors and support teams that are involved in the delivery of end-to-end IT services. More sophisticated communication and collaboration tools are needed to create fluid interactions with all parties involved. IT management tools need to be open to exchange data and provide integrations with other tools and external IT service providers.

Also keep in mind that a large amount of IT activities are performed or supported by specialized tools. For example, risk and Business Impact Assessments (BIA) are performed by a risk management system. Projects are managed in a project management system. For security monitoring, such as vulnerability management or intrusion detection, often specialized tools are needed; and, depending upon the specific technology such as Java or .NET, specific development and test management tools should be used. The result is a complex environment of tools and administrations to support the various IT management activities that cannot be easily integrated.

In addition, a large number of activities are outsourced to external vendors each using their own tools and processes. As a result, we need to build interfaces to effectively communicate and collaborate with these vendors. The benefit of using the IT4IT Reference Architecture is the implementation of an integrated and automated IT management environment to enhance the performance and maturity of the IT organization. Some examples of benefits of using the IT4IT approach for the IT organization itself are:

- The ability to implement the service broker and integrator role (consolidating component services from different external vendors).
- Lower costs by reducing the number of FTE needed to support IT services (due to automation of IT tasks, reduction of the number of incidents and

exceptions, etc.) and/or more time available to improve and enhance the IT service (instead of doing rework and performing firefighting activities).

- More flexible relationships with service providers (ability to plug-and-play service providers).
- Ability to optimize resource allocation by understanding all IT tasks to be performed for the business (managing an integrated backlog of tasks for the IT function).
- Ability to automate IT management tasks supporting end-to-end value streams (such as build, test, deployment automation, monitoring, discovery, and automated recovery).
- Improve the transparency of performance across different IT teams (and service providers). This can help to continuously improve the IT function by understanding why one team performs better than another team.
- Improve productivity of IT employees (by providing them the right information and support to optimize their IT work).
- Lower number of *ad hoc* or unplanned activities to be performed by IT specialists; resulting in less stress and higher employee satisfaction.
- Self-service capabilities that empower the IT employee to manage IT (for example, developers requiring temporary infrastructure resources such as servers and databases).
- Improved collaboration and communication between IT employees, business, and IT service providers.
- Ability to attract and retain the IT employees with the required new IT skills, competences, and attitude.

The IT4IT Reference Architecture also defines a standard information model to govern and manage IT information across the entire service lifecycle. This common data model has a number of benefits:

- Improved sharing of data/information and knowledge between involved stakeholders.
- Better decision-making due to improved data quality and availability of information; and ability to continuously improve IT services due to better insight.
- Easier to find information and generate reports (improved productivity and reducing the need to manually find and compile data).
- Cost transparency due to roll-up of consumption and costs data to IT services; and therefore providing the ability to reduce costs and eliminate waste.

- Ability to reduce costs due to better information about utilization of IT resources, available licenses, and workloads.
- Improved integration with external vendors to exchange information such as incidents, service requests, and configuration data.
- Reduced risks due to insight in security vulnerabilities, usage patterns, etc.
- Ability to identify rationalization opportunities due to better insight in the service portfolio.

Make IT flow – provide a single backlog for all IT tasks

IT employees are working on many different IT management activities, tasks, and backlogs. For example, in DevOps environments, employees perform both development and operations tasks.

The IT4IT approach is to define one logical platform to manage all IT tasks assigned to teams and IT specialists. This enables managing the flow of activities throughout the organization, assigning resources according to priority, available skills, and competences, and managing workloads.

Make IT Flow

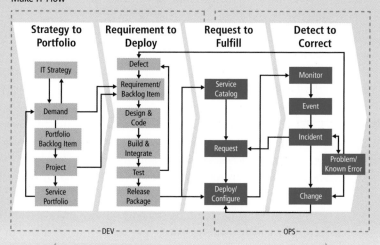

The volume of tasks managed and executed by an IT organization will grow significantly in the coming years. For example, due to Agile and Continuous Delivery practices which deliver more frequent releases and changes. The IT organization also needs to handle more service requests and respond to an increasing number of security events. More often these tasks are performed by a federation of IT service providers involved in the end-to-end service delivery.

The challenge is to manage all these different queues of tasks, prioritize and coordinate their execution, and assign the tasks to appropriate resources.

The idea is to create an integrated work queue (or backlog) supported by different systems such as Lean Kanban for the various type of activities within the IT organization such as:
- Demands (to be evaluated and prioritized)
- Portfolio backlog items
- Project management tasks
- Product backlog items
- Design and development tasks (driven by the product, sprint, and release backlog)
- Test tasks
- Defects (to be analyzed and resolved)
- Deployment tasks
- Service requests (and fulfillment tasks)
- Catalog maintenance tasks
- End-user support tasks (such as FAQ)
- Incident tasks
- Problem tasks
- Change tasks
- Change evaluation tasks
- Daily operations tasks (such as housekeeping, scheduled maintenance)
- Service reviews
- Audits and risks assessments
- ...

One of the key issues with the current IT operating models is the inadequacy of its IT information systems to provide all the necessary information to support decision-making and provide insight for continuous improvement. Information is not easily or readily available to IT employees to support their daily tasks. An IT specialist is typically dependent upon information managed in many different IT management systems and repositories. Effective decision-making depends upon consolidated and aggregated data from the different data sources. As a result, a lot of effort is needed to find and compile the required data to create insight. To resolve this challenge, the IT4IT standard defines a common information model for managing all IT data within the IT function.

4.2.3 The IT4IT Organization

This section provides an overview of the benefits of the IT4IT Reference Architecture for the organization and teams responsible for delivering IT management capabilities. The IT4IT organization (or function) is a logical entity that provides IT management best practices and standard tools. The IT4IT organization is continuously improving the way IT is managed and operated. This includes the IT4IT architect, IT4IT value stream owners, IT process owners, business analysts, IT tool specialists, IT process consultants, and so on (see Section 5.2 for more details).

The IT4IT organization is, for example, involved in the following activities:
- Define a way of working for IT processes (for example, related to Project Portfolio Management (PPM), test management, service catalog, incident, and change management) using common best practices and standards.
- Manage the portfolio of IT management tools.
- Select and implement IT management tools; for example, an ITSM system, CMDB or project management tool; providing an integrated IT management toolkit.
- Operate and support IT management tools (supporting all IT management tools within the IT organization).
- Train and educate IT specialists using the standard practices and tools.
- Develop interfaces between tools and external service providers (such as ticketing exchange).
- Define and develop standard IT management metrics and reports (such as SLA reports).

The IT4IT Reference Architecture provides an open standard to implement an end-to-end IT management system (consisting of multiple tools or products). This provides the opportunity to simplify, rationalize, and standardize the IT management tooling landscape. The market of IT management tools is still fragmented and in constant flux. At this moment there is no single vendor or solution that can fulfill all IT management requirements. Implementation of these solutions today typically requires a lot of design and configuration effort, specifically for customizing integrations between the different solutions to exchange data or automate workflows. Although tools typically support ITIL or SCRUM there is still a significant amount of work needed to make them production-ready. This is due to the fact that each vendor has implemented its own data model, workflows, and practices.

 The IT4IT Reference Architecture reduces the cost of building and maintaining an integrated IT management system by defining standard functional components, workflows, data models, and integration points.

The IT4IT Reference Architecture provides the ability to standardize and simplify the IT management landscape and deliver standard information models to exchange data. The IT organization should select and implement tools that support open standards such as the IT4IT standard. This improves the interoperability of IT management software from different solution vendors.

Most IT organizations do not have a dedicated team (or organization) responsible for all IT management processes and tools. For some standard solutions, such as the ITSM system and CMDB, a central support team is available. Typically, ownership of other IT management tools is embedded in different IT departments and teams. IT management tools are often implemented and managed by the IT operations staff or specialists themselves (also being the users). In addition to their busy work schedule managing IT services and providing support to the business, they also need to maintain the tooling landscape used to support their day-to-day activities. This distracts them from performing activities providing real business value – the delivery of added-value services to the business.

Compare this to a car manufacturer using a production facility with an assembly production line. Assembly workers focus on primary activities to build a car out of all the parts. They focus on creating value by producing cars. They should not be building and managing the assembly line itself with all the complexity of robotics and automation. In the IT function this assembly line can, for example, be compared with a continuous delivery tool-chain where requirements come into the backlog, application code is created by developers, build and integration is performed, test scripts are executed, and finally the release can be promoted into production. The developers and testers are creating value for the business, while IT4IT designs, configures, and maintains the assembly line – in this case the end-to-end IT4IT tool-chain needed to automate the IT lifecycle processes. Building this IT assembly line requires specialized skills and expertise of a large amount of tools and best practices such as related to requirements engineering, source code management, build and continuous integration, test automation, and deployment automation. The recommendation is to create an IT4IT organization (potentially a virtual entity) responsible for all IT management processes, data models, and tools. This IT4IT organization selects, implements, and maintains the IT management tools, while working in close collaboration and consultation with the IT specialists (the user community of IT management tools).

By organizing the IT4IT approach as a separate portfolio and assigning an IT4IT architect, the governance of IT management can be improved. Benefits of having an agreed IT4IT architecture and IT4IT management organization are:

- More control and governance on the selection of IT management tools to ensure fit into the overall architecture and roadmap.
- Improved prioritization (and return on investment) of IT management-related initiatives by providing a longer-term vision and roadmap; and the ability to continuously improve the IT management capabilities.
- Improved return on investment of available budget for IT management (tool and processes).
- Rationalized and simplified landscape of IT management tools needed to manage IT (reduced complexity of the entire IT management landscape).
- Getting more value from existing IT management tools (after rationalization and decommissioning of non-strategic tools).
- Ability to provide an integrated and unified IT management solution as a service to the IT function. Improved integration and data exchange between tools (due to standard information models and open interfaces).
- Reduce cost to implement and maintain IT management tools.
- Faster implementation of IT management capabilities due to using best practices and out-of-the-box integrations.
- Fewer risks when implementing (and integrating) new IT management tools.

- Less customizations and configuration changes needed due to open standards (resulting in lower costs and faster delivery). Select tools that have embedded the IT4IT standard and other best practices into a preconfigured solution.
- Less training needed to learn new tools and way of working.
- Provide a common terminology to discuss IT management capabilities with IT tool vendors, IT service providers, etc.
- Leverage best practices and standards in the market (and standard products and services from vendors).
- Ability to consume IT4IT capabilities as a service (IT4IT as a service) from IT solution vendors.
- Reduced vendor lock-in and dependency on IT management tool vendors (by enabling a more component-based solution and interoperability between tools).

The benefits of having a separate IT4IT organization responsible for the IT management tools include:
- IT employees such as developers and operations staff can focus on their primary production activities instead of maintaining and supporting the assembly line itself (the IT4IT management landscape). For example, developers want to write code, not manage the development tooling landscape.
- Leverage competences and skills to set up IT4IT capabilities across different IT departments and line of businesses (instead of each team to develop their own skills and competences to design, develop, and maintain IT management capabilities). Implementation of IT management tools, such as automation, becomes more complex and requires different skills and experience.
- Leverage best practices instead of each team reinventing the wheel (defining one way of working).

4.2.4 IT Service Providers
IT service providers are all IT organizations delivering market IT services (directly or indirectly) to the business. This includes, for example, hosting providers, network (or telecom) service providers, and various cloud vendors providing IaaS, PaaS, and SaaS services.

The benefits for the IT service providers are similar to those defined for the internal IT organization, whereby the IT4IT Reference Architecture provides a standard blueprint to optimize and streamline the IT service delivery through the entire lifecycle. Each service provider also has the challenge to develop and maintain interfaces between their IT management system(s) and the IT management systems of their customers. This is a complex assignment as each customer has different processes and tools.

Integration and data exchange between IT services providers and customers is one of biggest challenges. Most IT service providers have implemented their own proprietary integration platforms to exchange data with customers; for example, to:

- Receive incidents from customers (and provide status updates and resolutions)
- Synchronize service catalogs with customers
- Receive service requests
- Federate configuration data to/from customer CMDBs
- Exchange knowledge, known errors, and documents
- Publish SLA reports and supplier performance data
- Synchronize or publish the change and release schedule (for approval and impact assessment)
- Inform customers of major incidents (e.g., outages) or planned changes
- Provide consumption and cost data (billing and charging data and related evidence)
- Receive demand and project requests

The disadvantage of having these proprietary interfaces is that each integration with a new customer is very expensive and cumbersome. Often customers rely on manual integrations resulting in lower customer experience and more work on both sides. One of the biggest complaints related to outsourcing is the inability of service providers to provide relevant insight in the performance and costs of IT services delivered. This is mainly due to the lack of standard and open communication providing the ability to easily exchange information.

Using the IT4IT Reference Architecture integration and collaboration with customers can be improved significantly. Examples of benefits for the service provider include:

- Shorter time to on-board new customers (resulting in faster delivery and return on investment).
- Lower risks in outsourcing deals for the customer (resulting in shorter sales cycles).

- Reduced effort to implement integrations with different IT organizations (customers) by reuse of standard interfaces.
- Improved collaboration and communication with customers (resulting in higher customer satisfaction and loyalty).
- Ability to offer clients/customers a more comprehensive service as part of an IT4IT compatible ecosystem.
- Lower cost to maintain interfaces with the various customers; and to provide periodic reports and management information.

4.2.5   IT Management Software Vendors (or IT4IT Tool Vendors)

This section describes the benefits of adopting the IT4IT Reference Architecture for vendors providing IT management solutions. These software vendors develop and deliver standard IT management products (commercial off-the-shelf-software) to support various activities within the IT function. More often these IT management solutions are delivered as SaaS. In addition to these commercial products there are also a large number of open-source products available to support IT management activities.

In addition, technology vendors providing the core technologies such as servers, operating systems, database software, storage, networking, and other middleware also need to ensure their products can be managed and operated efficiently. These vendors also typically need to develop management capabilities as part of their technology offerings, and as such are also IT management product vendors.

There are many different types of IT management products available, such as project management software, development and test management tools, deployment automation tools, security management tools, Identity and Access Management (IAM) tools, IT Service Management (ITSM) systems, process and run book automation tools, monitoring tools and CMDB (see also Appendix C). Each vendor uses their own terminology and classifications to position their products. Adopting the IT4IT standard provides a standard structure, terminology, and classification scheme for mapping products to the functional components in the IT4IT Reference Architecture. This improves the visibility of how their offerings can fit into the overall IT management landscape of the IT organization.

Through the IT4IT Reference Architecture, software vendors, have access to a thoroughly designed end-to-end IT operating model that can be utilized and integrated into their own solutions at a lower overall cost. Using the IT4IT standard allows IT management software vendors to offer new and compelling value propositions to IT organizations and makes it easier for them to work with IT organizations to integrate their offerings into the entire IT management landscape.

Vendors of IT management solutions should adopt standards and best practices to reduce the time and effort needed to implement their software within an IT organization. This includes, for example, a standard information model, predefined workflows, preconfigured roles and responsibilities, standard reports, open interfaces, and so on. Unfortunately today most software products typically require a lot of design and configuration effort (and often a significant amount of customization) before they can be used effectively by the IT organization. In addition, building integrations between IT management tools also requires a lot of implementation effort. Upgrades to new versions often result in rework and frustration, and they take a long time. This is also the case for IT management solutions that are delivered as a service (SaaS).

Even though most tools do support a standard or common best practice such as PMBOK, ITIL, or SCRUM, there is still a significant amount of work needed to actually configure and integrate the product into a working solution. Each vendor has to implement their own data model, own workflows, and practices due to the fact that current frameworks, standards, and best practices such as ITIL are not prescriptive enough to build an actual working solution.

The IT4IT Reference Architecture provides this prescriptive architecture including a common data model and open standard interfaces. (The latter will be delivered as separate guides and white papers.) This reduces the effort of implementing and managing the IT management tools; and ensures interoperability between solutions provided by different IT management software vendors.

Possible adoptions by the IT management software vendor include:
- Map vendor solutions to the IT4IT value streams and functional components to provide more transparency of their service offerings.
- Support the standard IT4IT information model to enable data exchange.

- Build predefined workflows and functional capabilities as defined by the IT4IT Reference Architecture into their core product (for example, using end-to-end use-cases).
- Build standard reports based upon the standard KPIs and metrics.
- Provide open and standard interfaces according to the IT4IT standard to enable plug-and-play interoperability between products from different vendors.
- Active participation in The Open Group IT4IT Forum to co-design and develop the standard in more detail.
- Product certification – in due time, The Open Group is expected to offer certification of products, to ensure they are fit-for-purpose.

Software vendors who adopt the value stream approach are able to provide component-based solutions that enable an integrated end-to-end IT management landscape. Software vendors supporting the IT4IT standard will improve their ability to integrate with solutions from other vendors.

In summary, the benefits for IT management software (or solution) vendors adopting the IT4IT Reference Architecture are:
- Mapping of solutions to the IT4IT value streams and functional components provides their customers with more transparency and clarity to their product offerings.
- Speed up the sales cycle due to more confidence in the feasibility of the solution for the customer (using proven functionality); also reduce the risks associated with implementing their software into the IT management landscape of the customer.
- Differentiated service offering compared to vendors not supporting the IT4IT standard.
- Provide IT4IT capabilities as a standard service (IT4IT as a service).
- Innovate and compete on real customer added value while leveraging the IT4IT standard and compatible ecosystem.
- Use IT4IT standards and practices into preconfigured, re-usable software products and integrations reducing the effort to implement solutions for each customer.
- Simplified integration of their solutions with tools from other vendors (open standard integration).

- Easier upgrade of customers to the latest version due to less customization and configuration.
- Provide faster and enhanced return on investment for their customers.

4.2.6 Industry-Related Training and Certification Providers

A new market place is opening to offer training and education related to the IT4IT Reference Architecture. The Open Group is establishing a certification program for the IT4IT ecosystem. Industry standard certifications require a training curriculum that will provide the necessary knowledge for individuals to prove their knowledge and competence.

Chapter 5

How to Use the IT4IT Reference Architecture

This chapter describes how to get started with the IT4IT Reference Architecture. It provides high-level guidance of how to introduce the IT4IT approach within your own organization.

Key topics covered in this chapter:

- The use of IT4IT value streams and the IT4IT Reference Architecture as a diagnostic tool to assess the Current Mode of Operation (CMO) and identify improvement opportunities.
- The use of the IT4IT Reference Architecture to define the Future Mode of Operation (FMO); agreeing on the new IT operating model.
- A description of the overall governance model of managing IT4IT related practices.
- Guidance for building a business case for implementing the IT4IT Reference Architecture (using the benefits as presented in Chapter 4).
- An overall approach and roadmap to transition the IT function to the new IT operating model.
- Using the IT4IT Reference Architecture as a blueprint for discussing future IT management capabilities with IT management tool vendors (part of tool selection and vendor engagements).

5.1   Introduction

To improve the IT function (from where it is today) a fundamentally different approach is required to design, implement, and manage IT management capabilities. These IT management capabilities refer to processes, data, and solutions (and integrations) needed to run the IT function. The general idea behind the IT4IT approach is to provide the bigger picture of how to manage IT and how to improve the overall IT function by providing the right data and tools to automate end-to-end workflows. Instead of improving individual IT processes, tools, or capabilities, improve the overall chain or system.

> There is no shortcut to successfully transform the IT function. Starting
> with the IT4IT Reference Architecture will provide you with a complete
> picture and a concise framework for how the IT function should work.

A number of measures need to be taken to ensure IT4IT Reference Architecture
can be implemented within the IT organization. Key proposed measures are as
follows:

- Assign a lead IT4IT architect responsible for defining how IT is supported by
  the right solutions (covering process, data, tools, and integrations).
- Assign functional owners for each value stream (and related functional
  components and IT processes).
- Define IT4IT capabilities as a separate portfolio within the IT organization;
  this portfolio manages all IT4IT related applications, and assigns ownership
  of the IT4IT portfolio.
- Define consistent metrics and KPIs, which are relevant for managing the
  business of IT.
- Define a high-level blueprint of the target IT operating model (using the
  IT4IT Reference Architecture), including a proposed high-level roadmap.
- Define data owners of the information needed to manage the IT function (for
  example, define data dictionary, monitor data quality).
- Prioritize investments in IT management capabilities in line with the defined
  target architecture and agreed roadmap.
- Supervise and direct the selection of new IT management tools in alignment
  with the defined target architecture (preventing *ad hoc* tool selection).
- Set up a competence center to deliver and support the IT management
  tooling landscape.
- Make the IT4IT approach an important topic on the agenda of the CIO and
  executive management (to enable the new IT organization).
- Set up a competence model and training plan for acquiring IT4IT related
  expertise and skills.
- Use a maturity model to access the current maturity of IT4IT capabilities
  (as defined in the IT4IT Reference Architecture) to get to precise
  recommendations of what to improve.

Ownership of IT management tools and processes may have to be moved from
the different IT departments and operations teams to the IT4IT organization

(or competence center). For most IT organizations this is a completely different approach as compared to the current way of working:

- Different teams or departments select, implement, and manage their own set of tools and practices.
- Distributed ownership for IT management tools and processes (fragmented ownership of tools, processes, and data).
- No agreed and aligned IT4IT target architecture and related roadmap; as a result, decisions to invest in new tools or new capabilities are taken on an *ad hoc* basis.
- No common IT process framework covering all process and activities involved in portfolio management, development, and IT operations.
- Skills and competences related to IT management (e.g., practices such as SCRUM, test management, ITIL) and specialists of IT management tools are scattered throughout the organization.
- Lacking trusted data sources; fragmented data repositories; questionable data quality; lacking ability to consolidate data to support decision-making and provide transparency.
- Many different uncoordinated initiatives to modify/improve the IT management function (for example, enhance monitoring capabilities, security monitoring, CMDB, test automation, cloud provisioning, IAM, etc.).
- *Ad hoc* selection of IT management tools (such as new test management tools or migration to a new ITSM system).

As a result, a number of key challenges can be identified when the organization wants to implement an integrated IT4IT architecture, such as:

- Limited IT budget available for IT management process and tooling improvements
  Not much budget is allocated to the development of new IT management capabilities. Therefore, it would be good to reserve a specific percentage of each IT project to develop IT management capabilities.
- Transferring IT budget (for IT management process and tooling improvements)
  If budget is available within another business or department, it might be needed to transfer this budget to the IT4IT portfolio.
- Lacking central governance and ownership.
  Often the governance and ownership of IT management tools is fragmented throughout the IT organization. Different teams are responsible for their own

tools and processes. No central architecture or roadmap is defined to ensure IT4IT related investments are synchronized.

- No common agreed vision and IT strategy by higher management and IT management
  Due to the lack of a shared IT strategy and vision it is difficult to prioritize IT management initiatives. Adoption of the IT4IT standard by higher management and IT management is imperative.

- Legacy environments (and technology debt) require a need to fix first (reactive operations), thus having "keeping the lights on" behavior
  Different technology standards have been defined for IT. But often people did not adhere to these standards. As a result, the IT landscape has become too complex, often with many outdated (or near end-of-life) technologies that still need to be managed. Due to the lack of standards it becomes impossible to automate IT processes.

- Large investment in current IT management tools and practices
  IT management is not a greenfield. The current IT management estate consists of a complex set of IT processes and IT management tools, including interfaces with suppliers. There is not a simple roadmap or transition plan to move to a new more agile and simplified IT management system. In some cases a "greenfield" approach can be created when significant changes are taking place within the IT ecosystem, such as moving to cloud services.

- New delivery models or technologies impact the existing IT management landscape
  New delivery models such as using cloud and Software-Defined (SDx) will impact the IT management processes and tooling landscape. The challenge is to implement new management capabilities, while managing the current legacy services as well.

To successfully implement an IT4IT approach a number of additional risks need to be mitigated, as follows:

- The IT4IT approach has no priority on the CIO agenda (introducing new technologies and developing business applications have a higher priority). Implementing the capabilities to manage these new technologies is often neglected. Executive management needs to realize that building new IT management capabilities is vital to reap the benefits of new technologies such as mobility, cloud, or big data.

- No resources available (everybody is busy doing their own thing) with the right set of skills and expertise on IT management.

- Maturity of the IT management tool market (and required integrations); IT management tools often lack standard interfaces or capabilities to support the new IT.
- Teams do not believe a standard or central solution solves the problem. Typically, each department would like to retain control over their own processes and tools.
- Lacking standard integrations and data models to exchange data between tools and service providers (for example, exchange incidents, service requests, view consumption and costs of externals service providers).

A number of key success factors can be identified in order to mitigate the risks when implementing the IT4IT Reference Architecture, as follows:
- Understand the business vision and technology needs of the organization (new paradigms and new business demands).
- Define the IT strategy (and new technology vision) aligned with the business drivers and plans.
- Agree on using the IT4IT Reference Architecture as the overall model to design the IT management system.
- Take a holistic and end-to-end value stream approach (looking at the big picture first using the IT4IT value streams).
- Build a case for change using the IT4IT overall vision and reference model.
- Demonstrate the value of integrated IT management tools and processes using a "model office" (a kind of demo/lab environment for the IT employees to experience and influence the new way of working).
- Align the IT4IT roadmap with the IT strategy and vision.
- Ensure proper management of change, combining people, leadership, and cultural aspects in the approach.
- Have a good understanding of how IT is managed today (consisting of tools, data, processes, integrations, etc.).
- Ensure a sound management commitment and governance model.
- Have a good understanding of the art of the possible with current IT management software products (considering the maturity of IT management software products).

5.2   A High-Level Approach for Implementing the IT4IT Standard

This section describes a high-level approach for implementing the IT4IT Reference Architecture. It provides a series of steps that can be taken to implement IT4IT capabilities. As highlighted in previous sections, it is recommended to take a holistic approach looking at complete value streams instead of improving individual ITIL processes or functions.

Figure 24: High-Level Approach for Initiating the IT4IT Roadmap

This is a different approach than most of the improvement initiatives that an organization is currently undertaking. Every IT organization executes a large amount of initiatives to improve something within the IT function; such as improving test automation, performing tool selections, implementing deployment automation, improving the data quality of the CMDB, conducting a process maturity scan, organizing Agile or Lean training sessions, building reporting enhancements, and so on. Nowadays organizations use Continuous Improvement (CI) methods, Kaizen events, or apply other Lean practices. However, these approaches often have a limited scope (and time horizon) to review and improve an individual process, tool, or team. As a result, these *ad hoc* and fragmented initiatives will typically fail to deliver real value to the business. Improving each IT process or tool one-by-one (or at the same time) will not improve the overall performance of the IT organization.

Every IT organization has a large number of initiatives (often small-scale and uncoordinated projects), executed by different teams, to improve IT management capabilities. However, these fragmented projects and CI programs waste a lot of time and resources because they are not improving the end-to-end IT value delivery but rather sub-optimizing IT activities. It is wise to stop these fragmented initiatives and start with the development of a target state IT4IT architecture.

Because of all the inter-dependencies (as illustrated by the IT4IT value streams) the implementation and improvement of IT management requires a different approach. Instead of implementing quick-wins, CI, or fixes, the IT organization first needs to build a complete picture of the future IT operating model. You cannot continuously improve the IT organization or select new IT management tools if you don't have a vision on the target state IT operating model. Only with the overall IT4IT picture in mind can the end-to-end performance of the IT function start to improve.

Establishing an IT4IT capability is not just about the *toolset*, but more about the *mind set*.

To be successful, a different IT management governance model is needed of how IT management processes are designed and implemented, how tools are selected, or how new practices are rolled out. A vision of the future IT organization needs to be created first. For this new IT organization a target IT management backbone needs to be designed as well. Using this target model, a high-level roadmap can be created to define how to transition from the current to the future state. This requires a transition plan not only covering the processes and toolset, but also changing the mind set of people. New leadership structures, skills, and competences are needed. For example, new skills needed to implement the "service broker" function or new skills needed to automate and orchestrate IT activities, managing hybrid-clouds, and performing application release automation. These new IT4IT skills and competences need to be developed to successfully build and operate this new IT operating model.

The IT4IT approach provides the *backbone* to support all IT employees to perform their work more efficiently and effectively. It enables the IT organization to manage IT in a more simple, transparent, and integrated manner. By providing integrated tools and standard practices, an IT4IT approach can optimize the productivity of all IT staff, enabling the IT organization to automate IT management tasks, collaborate with the business more effectively, optimize the sourcing of services from IT service providers, and become more reliable, cost-effective, and innovate faster. It can also provide better communication and collaboration with the business (consumers of IT) by levering technologies such as self-service portals to order services and controlling IT consumption.

From a high-level perspective the following key activities need to be performed to implement the IT4IT vision:

1. Conduct IT4IT baseline assessment ("as-is" analysis):
   - Perform baseline assessment ("as-is" analysis and review) against the IT4IT Reference Architecture.
   - Build a complete picture of all current tools, processes, data, and controls defined to manage IT (and specifically identify end-of-life IT management tools or where contracts need to be renewed).
   - Capture all planned and active IT management-related initiatives or projects (specifically where new tools are selected or pilots are planned).
   - Initial understanding of gaps, issues, and challenges (building a case for change).
   - Identify key stakeholders (including those people with scarce skills and competences).
   - Preparation of a more detailed value stream analysis (next step).
   - Presentation for executive management explaining the need to build a blueprint for the target IT operation model.
   - Document what is going well and what needs to be improved.
2. Perform IT4IT value stream analysis:
   - Use the IT4IT value streams to perform a more detailed assessment and review of the current way of working within the IT organization.
   - Use storylines or use-cases to show how the current value streams are executed compared to the IT4IT Reference Architecture.

3. Define IT4IT ownership and governance model:
   - Set up an IT4IT governance model (and define ownership of this domain).
   - Assign key roles and responsibilities (such as assigning the IT4IT architect and IT4IT value stream owners).
   - Prepare a presentation for executives and key stakeholders.
   - Conduct initial training for the new appointed value stream owners (covering the IT4IT standard and other relevant best practices and standards).
4. Define IT management vision, mission, and strategy:
   - Define how the future IT organization looks; for example, becoming a service broker of a hybrid cloud service, self-service and high-level automation, implement DevOps, and so on.
   - Understand the IT strategy supporting the business strategy.
   - Understand and define the future role of the IT organization (in the digital transformation journey of the business).
   - Identify key IT services, technologies, and vendors.
   - Define the new technology strategy (for example, using hybrid-cloud, move to SaaS, and so on).
   - Identify skills needed for the new IT function (such as service catalog manager, cloud automation engineer, deployment automation specialist).
   - Create a motivational and inspiring story to explain how the new IT function will operate, and how exciting it would be to take part in that journey.
   - Create a simple presentation defining the vision, mission, and direction of the IT4IT approach (explaining the why and how).
5. Define the target IT4IT architecture (as part of the FMO):
   - Define the target state IT operating model (including goals, drivers) and the target IT management architecture for your organization.
   - Define the ambition level of each of the functional components (and IT4IT related capabilities).
   - Define end-to-end use-cases and scenarios (building storyboards) to illustrate how the new IT will be managed.
   - Select relevant standards, best practices, and frameworks to be incorporated under the IT4IT umbrella (such as the TOGAF standard, ITIL, PMBOK, and SCRUM).
   - Define strategic vendors as part of the IT4IT ecosystem (vendors for the IT management capabilities such as tool vendors).

6. Perform gap analysis:
   - Perform gap analysis of the current situation (and its key functional components) against the target model.
   - Score current IT management capabilities (considering the defined IT management vision and ambition levels).
   - Identify gaps (for example, skills/competences, attitude and mind set, processes, tool capabilities, data).
   - Identify quick-wins and rationalization opportunities (for example, consolidate different service management tools).
   - Document gaps, outstanding questions, and issues.
7. Define roadmap and business case:
   - Build the IT4IT roadmap (high-level).
   - Engage with business stakeholders and IT management tool vendors to validate and confirm the roadmap.
   - Identify and prioritize investments.
   - Build the business case (and confirm reason for change).
8. Set up an IT4IT model office:
   - Set up a model office as a controlled environment where IT staff and stakeholders can experience the benefits of an integrated approach to IT management (as a kind of IT4IT experience center).
   - Use this environment as a development and test environment for IT4IT capabilities.
9. Initiate and execute the IT4IT transformation roadmap:
   - Perform Change Readiness Assessment (CRA).
   - Define overall IT4IT program and transition plan.
   - Build the IT4IT portfolio.
   - Fund the IT4IT portfolio.
   - Perform pilots and tool selections (using the IT4IT Reference Architecture as the blueprint).
   - Promote culture of innovation and experimentation using IT4IT architectural guidance.
   - Implement the IT4IT architecture using an iterative approach.
   - Develop an IT4IT staffing and resource plan. Build competences and skills needed to manage the new IT4IT toolset.
   - Continuously improve the IT4IT architecture (ensure continuously captured feedback for both IT specialists as business stakeholders).

The above highlighted approach suggests a large transformation program to move to a new IT operating model. However, even if it is not feasible to initiate such a transformation journey, it is still essential to complete most of the above-defined steps. An IT organization should define an overall IT4IT architecture or blueprint providing guidance for future projects. This at least requires an architecture role taking accountability and ownership of the IT4IT segment. For this an IT4IT architect is assigned who will work with the different businesses and stakeholders on defining the target state architecture for the IT management function. Even if the ownership of IT management processes and tools remains distributed in the IT organization, central architectural governance is needed to provide the guidance and steer to align all projects and initiatives according to the overall IT4IT vision.

The execution of the above defined activities results in a number of essential deliverables. Some key deliverables of the IT4IT transformation include:
- IT4IT baseline assessment results
- IT4IT application portfolio list (current list of IT management tools/repositories)
- IT4IT related projects and initiatives (identified IT management improvement projects, tool selections, process improvements, and so on)
- IT4IT governance model
- IT4IT skills and competences matrix (overview of new roles and responsibilities within the new IT operating model)
- IT4IT stakeholder map (identify all stakeholders for IT management)
- IT management strategy, mission, and vision (and defined benefits)
- IT4IT gap analysis
- IT management organization diagram
- IT4IT target architecture
- IT4IT roadmap and high-level program plan with a related business case(s)

The following sections explain these above-mentioned activities in more detail.

5.2.1   Conduct IT4IT Baseline Assessment

It is imperative to get a good understanding of how the IT function is currently organized and how IT services are managed throughout the entire service lifecycle. The only way to improve IT management is to understand the bigger picture first. The IT4IT value streams should be the starting point to perform a structural analysis of the current tools, processes, data, integrations, and people involved in end-to-end workflows. The IT4IT Reference Architecture defines all required capabilities of the IT function, which offers a practical tool to support this exercise and diagnose the current way of working. This approach takes a holistic view from an end-to-end perspective, so not focusing on specific departments, technologies, teams, processes, or functions such as project management, service development, test management, service monitoring, incident management, or configuration management.

Start with a good understanding how IT is managed today ...
Most CIOs and IT managers do not have a good understanding how IT is actually managed from a day-to-day perspective. Typically, an overview of all practices and IT management tools used to support IT processes is missing. Although there are standard ITIL processes and tools implemented, you will be surprised how many additional practices are used by IT employees (a kind of shadow IT4IT capability).

If you take the time and effort to look at how the current IT function is organized (and supported by IT management tools) you will be daunted and surprised. You will see that there are so many different tools (and spreadsheets) but so less information and insight.

Do you have an overview of all IT processes defined in the IT organization? What are the key metrics and KPIs to manage the IT organization? What data is needed for managing IT (and where is it mastered)? Is there an overview of all processes and activities involved from an end-to-end value stream perspective; for example, from a new demand from the business to the actual release of the solution in production? How are these end-to-end workflows supported by tools? How do you collaborate and integrate with the different service providers; for example, exchange incidents and changes? How are costs assigned to applications and consumers?

The IT4IT Reference Architecture provides the blueprint that can be used to perform the baseline assessment to understand how IT is currently managed compared to the IT4IT standard.

Your story?

As the new CIO of a large company, the board of directors has sent you on a mission to significantly lower costs, increase efficiency, and speed up delivery. You are excited to start and keen to succeed. After thoroughly analyzing the current IT landscape you have come to the conclusion that it is far from ideal.

To service the business, the IT organization uses a rather complex system of integrated components and many more tools than absolutely necessary. In addition, several department managers have complained about inconsistent and unreliable data due to too many data sources. It seems that no one in the IT function has a good end-to-end understanding of how IT is currently managed, what tools are used, how they are integrated, and where the data is mastered.

Hence, after consulting with various parties, you have come to the conclusion that adopting the IT4IT approach helps you tackle many, if not all issues. So you decide to set up a special IT4IT program aimed to introduce standardization and at the same time reduce the overall complexity, number of interfaces, and tool customization.

The baseline assessment is used to perform a rough investigation of the current IT management landscape within a few weeks. A limited number of resources are needed to perform this activity; and the outcome can be used to convince stakeholders to continue with a further investigation using a more detailed value stream analysis.

Below is an overview of activities as part of the assessment:
- Identify all formally defined IT processes (and its process owners and practice leads). Collect all formal process documentation and relevant reference materials.
- Map the identified IT processes to the IT4IT value streams and supporting activities.
- Identify key stakeholders and lead practitioners involved in the architecture, design, and delivery of IT management capabilities (to create a stakeholder map).

- Identify all standards and best practices used by IT such as ITIL, COBIT, PMBOK, and SCRUM.
- Identify current key controls, metrics, and reports (as defined and used to manage IT today).
- List formal defined job profiles and related skills/competency levels (if available).
- Conduct an inventory of all IT management tools and identify tool owners (as part of the IT4IT portfolio) and map these tools to functional components from the IT4IT Reference Architecture.
- Investigate how each functional component as defined in the IT4IT Reference Architecture is implemented (and supported by standard tools, best practices, etc.).
- Assess the maturity of each functional component as defined in the IT4IT Reference Architecture (high-level understanding of how this is implemented within the IT function and how well it is working).
- Compile a list of all improvement initiatives, projects, or changes related to IT management that are planned or are in-flight within the different IT departments and teams (including the project sponsor and other relevant stakeholders).
- Identify all (or planned) tool selections or pilots (or other vendor engagement activities) related to IT management such as tool selection for monitoring, CMDB, ITSM, etc.
- Identify stakeholders involved in the investigation or implementation of new IT management practices such Agile, Lean IT, DevOps, or Continuous Delivery.
- Identify owners of the data within the IT function (using the IT4IT data objects) including the mapping to the master data repository (based upon the inventory of all IT management tools).
- Build a list of key vendors involved in the delivery or support of IT management activities.
- Identify the key external service providers (or vendors) involved in development and daily supporting activities; also check with these vendors whether they use their own processes and tools.
- Identify key integrations of the IT organization with external service providers (and how these are performed; e.g., manual or through automated integrations).

Are you in control?

Key questions you should ask yourself are: How do we manage IT today? Are we really in control?

If you are in control, you should be able to easily find the information to answer the following questions (without having to perform a time-consuming analysis):

- What IT services/applications do we have in the IT portfolio? What opportunities are available for rationalization and simplification?
- What does each IT service/application cost to run and maintain (based upon actual IT resource usage, license costs, support staff costs, contracts, etc.)?
- Who is subscribed to each IT service/application (list of all users per application and their access rights)?
- How well is each IT service performing against the SLA and business expectations? What are the outstanding problems that need to be resolved?
- How does the business perceive the value of each IT service? How satisfied is the business with the delivered service?
- What projects or initiatives are planned (funnel or in-flight) for each application (project portfolio)?
- What requirements (or user stories) are in the product backlog for each service?
- What IT resources (such as servers and databases) does each IT service/application use (basically do we know the service model of an application in the CMDB)?
- What are the risks and issues with each IT service/application?
- What are the business demands for new or modified services/applications (as part of the portfolio backlog)?

Typically, these above questions are not easy to answer. To answer these questions, data from different IT administrations, teams, and processes needs to be reconciled.

Other questions to ask yourself:

- How much are we dependent upon manual activities? Should we not automate more IT activities?

- Do we have sufficient self-service and self-help capacities in place? How much of standard activities such as service requests are automated?
- Can we find the right information at the right time (easy access to information) to support IT management decisions? How much effort does it take to search for information to get the required insight?
- Are we dependent upon the user to tell us something went wrong? Should we not improve our monitoring capabilities?
- Do we prevent incidents? Do we have sufficient proactive problem management in place?
- How well do we communicate with the business when there is an incident or outage?
- Do we know whom to contact in case of incidents or questions? Does the user know whom to contact?
- Do we have a standard funnel to capture all demands and ideas?
- Are we well equipped to continuously improve the IT organization?
- How much effort do we need to create monthly reports? Do these reports help to improve IT?
- Are we ready to manage new IT technologies such as cloud, mobility, and big data?
- How do we know we invest in the rights applications/projects to deliver business value?

The IT4IT Reference Architecture is used as the overarching framework to structure the content and to ensure all IT activities are considered in the baseline assessment. The following deliverables are the outcome of the baseline assessment:

- Inventory of IT management tools (and the data managed by these tools), including involved tool vendors, implementation partners, and support parties
- List of identified IT processes (and potential different versions or flavors per department)
- Mapping of tools to IT4IT value streams and the IT4IT Reference Architecture (and functional components)
- Stakeholder map (key stakeholders identified per tool, process, or value stream)
- Overview of initial findings and issues (for example, functional components not implemented or without formal tools)

- Overview of all planned or in-flight IT management initiatives/projects or improvement actions (as well as all tool selections and/or vendor engagements)
- List of key external service providers involved in the IT management ecosystem
- High-level picture of the current IT management blueprint (mapped onto the IT4IT Reference Architecture)

Build a complete IT4IT tool inventory

Do not underestimate the number of tools your IT organization is using to support the different activities within the value streams. Most IT organizations do not have a complete overview of all IT management solutions implemented within their IT organization. Appendix C provides an example of tool categories, which can be used as a reference to conduct an inventory of all IT management tools.

Examples: project management system, service desk/helpdesk system, CMDB, monitoring and event management tools, discovery tools, software asset management, project, Enterprise Architecture tools, development and test tools, security management tools, and so on. Often, for each technology vendor in use within an IT organization, additional vendor-specific management tools are used.

The applications used to support IT processes should be registered in a service/application portfolio.

Once an initial inventory of IT management applications is performed, additional information can be collected through interviews and reviews such as:

- Who owns the application? Who is using the application?
- Who is the vendor of application (or is it custom-built)?
- Which processes and IT4IT functional components does it support?
- How well does the application support the IT management activities?

- What data does the application manage (mastership of data)?
- What standard reporting capabilities are available?
- What is the level of customization (e.g., out-of-the-box, custom built, standard package with minor customizations)?
- Are there any risks or problems with the application (e.g.. security risks, compliance, technology debt, stability, performance, etc.)?
- How is the application delivered and supported (e.g., SaaS or internally hosted)?
- When is the application end-of-life? Is there a need for upgrade or replacement?
- What are the contracts related to the application (e.g., end-date or renewal dates)?
- What are the estimated yearly costs to run and maintain the application?
- What are the key challenges and problems with using the application?
- What changes or initiatives are planned affecting these IT management applications?
- How many users? Who are the users of the application (e.g., all IT employees, specific departments or specific roles, etc.)?
- What are the key integrations with other applications and external service providers?
- How easy is the application to use? How easy is it to maintain and upgrade?
- How well can the application integrate with other systems or reporting tools (e.g., does it support REST APIs)? Does it have an open data model import and export data?
- How strategic is the application and vendor of the solution? How well does the application and vision of the vendor fit into the IT4IT architecture and IT management vision of the organization?

It is important to map all IT management tools to the different value streams as well as to the functional component parts of a value stream. For example:

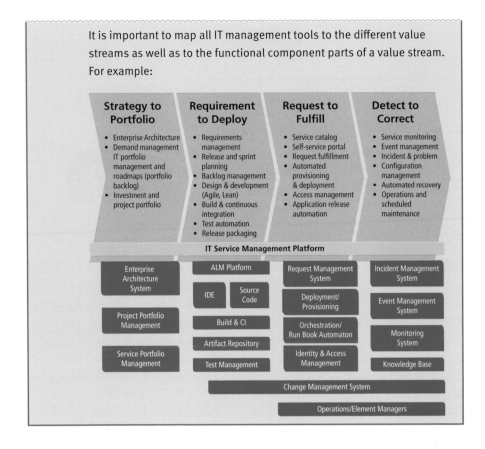

A key activity in the baseline assessment is to compile a complete inventory of all IT management-related tools and administrations used by the IT function. This includes custom-built solutions and standard software packages, and even vital spreadsheets that might be used to support IT. The IT4IT Reference Architecture can be used as a checklist to structure and guide this inventory. Creating such an inventory is not a simple task as it is also important to understand how well each IT solution is used, whether it is a commercial off-the-shelf package or custom build, and so on. Not many people (probably none) have a complete and good overview of all IT management tools used by the different IT departments supporting the various processes.

Three different perspectives will be encountered, as illustrated in Figure 25. First, how do people think IT is managed? Second, how is IT actually performed? And finally, build the new model of how we should manage IT.

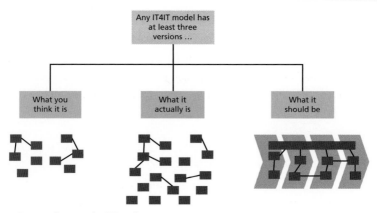

Figure 25: Perspectives on the IT Landscape

Often there is an overly optimistic view of how well things are managed today; therefore, it is important to validate how IT is actually performing. This can be confirmed by performing a "go and see" which is an action of going to see the actual process, understanding the work, asking questions, and learning from the people executing the day-to-day activities. But even if IT is managed appropriately today (although that is really rare), there is probably still a need to change and prepare for the new IT. The IT ecosystem will radically change and so must IT management. There is a need to automate more IT activities (such as testing, deployment, monitoring, and automated operations; as well as improving self-service and self-help capabilities), implement Agile practices, Continuous Delivery, and implement the service broker role, orchestrating services from external service providers.

Inventory of all IT management initiatives/projects
During the baseline assessment it is important to identify all currently proposed, planned, or in-flight projects (or initiatives) to improve the IT management function. This includes projects such as:
- IT process improvements
- New IT management tool selections or pilots
- Vendor engagements (of IT tool vendors, IT management consultancy)
- Planned migrations of existing tools to new solutions (e.g., migrate to a new service desk tool)
- Training plans for new IT skills (such as Agile, SCRUM)
- Reporting initiatives (such as scorecards)

- Market research activities (such as how to manage cloud vendors)
- Re-organizations (new roles and responsibilities)
- Implementation of new methods such as Agile, Lean, and SCRUM
- Continuous improvement projects
- Licenses (or contracts) to be renewed for IT management tools
- Demonstrations and planned vendor sessions

Typically, a large number of initiatives are planned or running scattered throughout the IT organization, such as:

- Implementing new security monitoring tools (such as vulnerability scanning)
- Application performance monitoring (or end-to-end/business chain monitoring)
- Improve Identity and Access Management (IAM)
- Improve reporting solution (such as SLA reporting, IT data warehouse)
- CMDB data quality improvements
- Cost management/cost transparency project
- Investment planning
- New Project Portfolio Management (PPM) system
- Test automation
- Security testing
- Operations data analytics
- Continuous Integration (CI) and continuous delivery tool-chain (or pipeline)
- Automated inventory/discovery
- Self-service portal and request management system
- Software license management initiative (and software scanning)
- Implement cloud management capability
- Application Release Automation (ARA)
- Investigate operations data analytics tools (for example, log file analytics)
- Investigate proactive monitoring and trend analysis
- Implement management tools as part of new technologies (such as converged infrastructure stacks)
- (and many more)

> Building this list of initiatives and improvements (and their budgets) is essential to understanding what changes are planned (or needed). The next step would be to position all these initiatives in an overall IT4IT roadmap to ensure alignment with the (to be defined) target reference architecture.
>
> This potentially also means that current tool selections need to be postponed until there is an agreed target blueprint (again: start with the big picture first).

5.2.2   Perform IT Value Stream Analysis

After the baseline assessment has been performed, a more detailed walkthrough is needed using the IT4IT value streams as guidance. This section provides a short overview of how to perform the value stream analysis to get a better understand of how IT activities are actually executed on a day-to-day basis. The supporting activities as part of the IT Value Chain are also part of this analysis.

 Value stream analysis
Follow a "product" or "service" from beginning to end, and draw a visual representation of every process in the material and information flow.

The basic idea of the value stream analysis is to validate how end-to-end activities (using a number of scenarios or use-cases) are supported by tools and what information is used. In addition, this detailed walk-through also captures:

- Activities performed (workflow) (mapped to the formal documented IT processes if available)
- Input (and output) (what is the outcome and value) such as formal deliverables or products delivered
- Data (information) used or needed
- Involved teams
- Roles and responsibilities (and related skills/competences)
- Tools used to support or automate the tasks
- Interfaces between systems and/or vendors
- Control points (specific controls and checks defined)
- Define metrics/KPIs to monitor the performance and quality
- Reports used to manage the operational, tactical, and strategic processes

A critical success factor to enable change is to first understand the current way of working ... It is also imperative that the current state or "as-is" is clearly understood before change is promoted. This analysis must be based on fact and not opinion.

Therefore, invest time in a "day in the life" (go and see) of an IT specialist, observing their patterns and behaviors, approaches, and processes, in the context of their world.

It is critical to success to clearly define the need for change and to check if it is real.

The value stream analysis should be performed by using a number of use-cases (or scenarios), which are related to the different IT4IT value streams. Examples of use-cases are:

- Strategy to Portfolio: New business demand to modify an existing IT service.
- Requirement to Deploy: New requirement to be delivered in the next release of an application.
- Request to Fulfill: User requesting a standard product from the catalog (from request to the actual fulfillment of the request).
- Request to Fulfill: User requesting access to a business application (from request to the actual fulfillment of the request).
- Request to Fulfill: IT specialist requesting a server or database from the infrastructure service catalog (from request to the actual fulfillment of the request).
- Detect to Correct: Event or exception detected by a monitoring tool (from detection to resolution).

The value stream analysis follows the use-case (related to a product or service) from beginning to end, and draws a visual representation of every activity in the end-to-end workflow.

The power of value stream storytelling

A good method to explain the challenges of IT management and the role of the IT4IT approach is using *storytelling*. Storytelling is used to support the management of change and initiate the transition.

Define a number of core use-cases per value stream which can be used to analyze the current way of working but also to describe how we envision the new way of working. For example, imagine:
- Business raises a demand for a new or modified IT service.
- Someone has a good idea for a new service or improvement.
- A stakeholder raises a new requirement to be implemented.
- An IT developer orders a new server or database.
- An end-user request a product from the service catalog.
- An outage or performance degradation is detected affecting the service delivered to the business.
- A security vulnerability is detected. (How is this handled and resolved?)
- ...

As preparation for the value stream analysis, use the outcome of the baseline assessment, and use the documented IT processes and procedures relevant for the value streams. The value stream analysis will highlight some gaps and differences of the actual workflow *versus* documented IT processes.

The analysis also validates and enriches the IT management tool inventory (and repositories) used to support IT management-related activities including homegrown solutions, document management/collaboration platforms, reporting solutions, and even important spreadsheets.

The analysis will also identify non-standard or local systems used by specific teams or support parties. Even when there are standard solutions defined for the entire IT organization, such as for test management or CMDB, it is important to verify how these solutions are actually used – and whether all teams or projects use them. Often teams or departments have implemented their own additional shadow administrations or built their own add-on solutions ("shadow IT4IT") instead of using the standard enterprise solution.

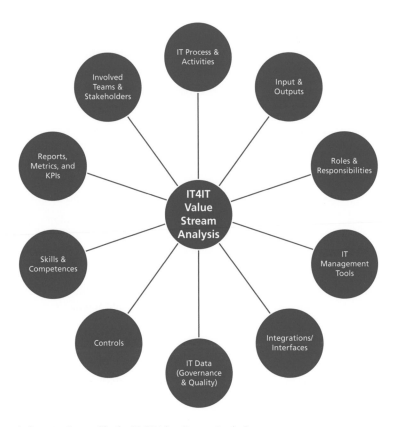

Figure 26: Aspects Covered in the IT4IT Value Stream Analysis

Do the test on a whiteboard ...

A good method to understand how well the end-to-end processes are defined and used today, is to ask key stakeholders to draw the following scenarios on a whiteboard:

- Demand for a new service from initiation to actual release in production
- Demand for an enhancement to an existing service from initiation until released
- Request standard end-user service from the catalog (such as new laptop or access to a business application) from request to fulfillment
- Request standard infrastructure service from the catalog (such as new server or database)
- Incident detected by an end-user from detection to resolution
- Incident detected by monitoring tools from detection to resolution

For each scenario above ask a person to draw the end-to-end process; and ask them to define what tools are used, what information is captured (and where), and check whether this procedure is valid for all IT services or only for specific technologies or teams, how information is shared with other systems or teams, and how tasks are assigned, and so on.

You will probably find out that none of the stakeholders have the desired end-to-end picture of how IT is actually working today. Each stakeholder often has a different understanding of activities that are performed (in contrast to the formal agreed process – if even documented).

An alternative approach is to ask a number of key stakeholders (or teams) to prepare a short presentation covering a walk-through of a few relevant end-to-end use-cases. Then organize a joint session to present each version of the truth; and with this input compile an integrated storyline of how the use-cases are supported by the IT organization today.

After these sessions, perform a number of "go see" or gemba walks to understand how the work is actually performed. This will probably result in many surprises, where things work differently per team, department, or service.

In the value stream analysis it is important to understand exactly how "work" and "tasks" that deliver value to a business (typically related to a specific product or service) are performed. It must be clear how work is pushed (or preferably pulled) through the value stream, as illustrated in Figure 27.

A number of methods can be used in this value stream analysis to collect data, such as:
- Go see and gemba walks
- Questionnaires and web-based surveys
- On-site interviews – interviews with IT personnel can enable assessment personnel to collect useful information about the IT4IT system (e.g., how the system is operated and managed)
- Document review (such as process documentation, user manuals)
- Use of automated scanning tool (to discover all IT management tools used by the IT organization)

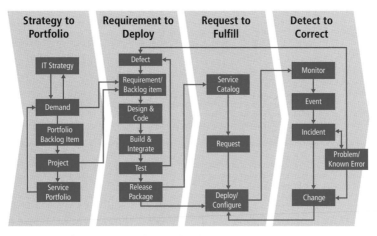

Figure 27: Connecting the Dots Across the IT Value Chain

- Check usage of standard templates (such as project plan templates, test plans, …)
- Perform a maturity scan of IT4IT related capabilities
- Identify waste in the value streams (by applying Lean methods and Six Sigma practices)
- Analyze actual data and review reports – review actual data from IT management tools such as incidents ticket analysis, view product backlog, project list, planned changes (or change calendar), service catalog, and so on

Gemba Walk (or Gemba)

In lean manufacturing, the idea of gemba is that the problems are visible, and the best improvement ideas will come from going to the *crime scene* (or workfloor). The gemba walk, much like Management By Walking Around (MBWA), is an activity that takes management to the front lines to look for waste and identify improvement opportunities. Gemba walks denote the action of going to see the actual process, understanding the work, asking questions, and learning. [Source: Wikipedia]

One of the risks of using gemba is that practitioners often "zoom" in too much on specific topics – as a result, the end-to-end picture is lost and improvements initiated do not improve the overall end-to-end performance. The advice is to focus on the end-to-end use-case from a value stream perspective and follow the entire flow. Typically, continuous improvement activities fall into this trap by limiting the scope and

> focusing on individual processes or teams with the idea to implement quick-wins and fix the process. For example, only focus on a specific function or capability such as test management, deployment automation, configuration management, and incident management. The will only result in a sub-optimization of these individual processes and not improving the IT management function. Again, start with the end-to-end big picture first ...

5.2.2.1 Strategy to Portfolio

The Strategy to Portfolio (S2P) value stream provides all the capabilities needed to manage the portfolio of services fully aligned with business goals and plans. Note that S2P manages all strategic and tactical demands to continuously optimize the IT service portfolio. Operational demands such as service requests are managed through the Request to Fulfill (R2F) value stream.

Often an IT organization does not have a standardized process and tool to manage the funnel of all types of demands linked to the services within the portfolio. Also the prioritization and initiation of projects are not very well defined and governed. All investment proposals and demands need to be related to IT services in the portfolio to determine the impact and potential benefits.

Typical issues or challenges that are revealed during the analysis of this value stream are:
- No central repository of all IT services and applications (and associated roadmaps).
- Lacking single funnel to manage demands, evaluate, and initiate projects.
- Difficult to prioritize investments aligned with business plans and technology roadmaps.
- Lacking ability to monitor benefits realization (of investments).
- Wrong investment decisions; investing in applications/services not delivering the expected value (or projects had to be cancelled).
- No budget available to perform the necessary upgrades and technology refresh (resulting in technology debt).
- No balanced investment between innovation (providing new capabilities), enhancements or improvements to existing services, and necessary technology refresh (such as upgrades).
- No clearly defined processes for IT service, investment, and PPM.

- Missing link between projects and IT services (or applications) (no transparency of project delivery).

During the assessment it is important to check whether these issues are also applicable to your own IT organization.

5.2.2.2 Requirement to Deploy

IT organizations today experience challenges in planning, sourcing, developing, and delivering applications and services that generate desired business outcomes. The Requirement to Deploy (R2D) value stream is designed to ensure predictable, cost-effective, high-quality results to the business while also promoting high levels of re-use, flexibility, speed, and collaboration across IT to support traditional and new methods for service creation and sourcing.

The R2D value stream provides all the capabilities needed to build and deliver IT services aligned with the business requirements and conform to IT policies and standards. This value stream ensures the service is developed (or configured) to fulfill the business requirements, as well as in conformance with non-functional requirements such as related to performance, maintainability, and security.

In addition, this value stream supports different type of service development scenarios such as:
- Custom code development (for example, .NET and Java applications)
- PaaS application development (for example, Force.com or Microsoft Windows Azure)
- Traditional package-based software development such as ERP or CRM software
- SaaS applications (even SaaS application-specific requirements need to be configured)
- Infrastructure service development (for example, a new IaaS service or new hosting platform, storage management service, and so on)

Note: R2D not only manages software development. Any service including infrastructure services are design, developed, and tested using the same functional components.

Different development methods can be used in the R2D value stream such as Waterfall or Agile development practices (for example, using SCRUM).

Typical gaps in this value stream:

- Lacking proper requirements management capability (and collaboration with stakeholders to validate requirements). Requirements are managed in spreadsheets.
- No formal product backlog with all requirements as needed by the business.
- No communicated release plans (with stakeholders).
- No transparency of which requirements are delivered in which release.
- No central repositories for source code control.
- Lacking integration of defects to incident and problem functional components.
- Manual build and test activities.
- Incomplete test management activities (resulting in failed changes or incidents in production).
- Lacking traceability from requirement, development, build, test, to deploy.
- Long lead time to deliver a small enhancement or change to the business (actual release into production).
- Design documentation not up-to-date or missing.
- Manual deployment activities.
- Development of features and functions not used in production (or not having the expected business benefit).
- No link from the development and test management system to the PPM system (no transparency of the progress).
- A lot of rework due to incorrect design.
- Delay of development and test activities due to late or unavailable test servers (long delivery time).
- Many different tools used by different development teams (each team or even person comes with their own toolset).
- Lacking development standards for specific IT management tasks such as logging, monitoring, operations tasks, security, and access management.
- Unused capacity due to test management servers running without any load (or usage) (just waiting for the next release).
- End-to-end process is not transparent for stakeholders and end-users.
- Lacking insight and reports to improve the performance of the development and test activities (and external vendors involved in this process).

In the detailed assessment of the R2D value stream it is important to validate and verify what capabilities have been implemented such as:

- Requirements management

- Prototyping and design tools
- Manage product backlog
- Development standards
- Source code management
- Build automation
- Test management (managing test cases, test plans)
- Security testing
- Performance and load testing
- Test data management
- Service virtualization
- Test automation
- Defect management
- Software packaging
- Document management
- Release and deployment automation

Examples of new practices the IT organization needs to evaluate (or is working on):
- Continuous Integration (CI) and continuous delivery
- Requirement engineering and specification
- Agile and Lean software development
- Mobile development
- Test automation
- Test data management
- Test-Driven Development (TDD)
- Security testing and code analysis
- Application release automation

5.2.2.3 Request to Fulfill

The Request to Fulfill (R2F) value stream provides all the capabilities needed to request and provide a consumable service linked with service usage and charging. The R2F value stream manages the service catalog and subscriptions of users to these services. This includes:
- Maintenance of the service catalog
- Provide self-service portal to handle all service requests
- Support approval workflow
- Coordinate and orchestrate the fulfillment of requests (preferably fully automated)

- Integrate with external service providers
- Manage subscriptions and access rights of users to services
- Monitor actual service usage and costs
- Automatically update the CMDB and other administrations based upon request fulfillment activities
- Provide show-back (or chargeback) of consumption and costs to the user
- Cancel a subscription or request decommission of IT resources

During the analysis of this value stream a number of typical gaps can be identified, such as:
- No standard documented and published IT services catalog.
- No standard fulfillment plans for recurring/standard requests.
- No charging for IT services to their actual service usage.
- Service fulfillment execution is mostly performed manually.
- Long lead (and wait) times from request to actual fulfillment (a standard request can take many weeks with only a few hours of man hours actually spent on the request).
- CMDB not automatically updated during or after provisioning.
- No software license verification possible prior to deployment.
- New infrastructure components deployed without linking to the correct application or service (for example, missing link between servers or databases to the application).
- Lots of errors and rework as a result of incorrectly executed fulfillment run books.
- No central administration of all users subscribed to the different IT services (subscription administration).

Because requests are processed in large volumes and are typically repetitive, it is required to define standard workflows and activities to fulfill each request from the catalog. These workflows are very complex; for example, think about all activities to be performed when requesting a new virtual server:
- Network management activities, such as defining the server's IP address, VLAN, domain name, etc.
- Provision the server using a standard image on a virtualization platform
- Configure the server by installing additional software (network settings, install monitoring agents, backup procedure, etc.)
- Install required patches/fixes (since creation of last image)

- Configure firewall rules
- Provide access to server (for specific administrators or users)

A number of capabilities need to be reviewed and validated as part of the value stream, for example:
- Service catalog
- Self-service portal
- Approval workflows
- Automated provisioning of service requests
- Automatically update the CMDB and license administration
- Subscription administration
- Integration with IAM systems (e.g., user identities and access rights)
- Customer survey tools (after request fulfillment)
- Orchestration and deployment automation tools
- Reporting tools
- Software metering; or monitor actual usage
- Showback/charge back tools
- Technology-specific management tools (such as network management, system management, storage management, database management)

The R2F value stream is also dependent upon the infrastructure and technology strategy. For example, new technologies typically introduce new deployment and management capabilities such as:
- Cloud provisioning and management
- Converged infrastructure (a single stack managing storage, compute, and network)
- Software-Defined Network (SDN) (or Software-Defined Data Center)
- New deployment methods, such as using containers

5.2.2.4 Detect to Correct
The Detect to Correct (D2C) value stream provides all the capabilities needed to ensure continuous operations of IT services according to agreed service levels. D2C covers a broad range of activities to operate IT services:
- Support end-users reporting incidents (through self-service portal).
- Monitor and detect exceptions; and resolve incidents (preferably before the business is affected).
- Monitor and act upon security events and vulnerabilities.

- Monitor performance and capacity usage; and continuously tune and improve performance.
- Actively modify IT resource allocation according to policies and budget constraints (e.g., reducing over-capacity).
- Monitor configuration changes against policies and formally approved changes (e.g., identify unauthorized changes).
- Monitor access of users and systems to IT services; identify unauthorized access or usage of IT services.
- Perform proactive problem management activities to prevent incidents and outages for the business.
- Perform patch management and daily house-keeping activities to ensure continuous operations.
- Monitor scheduled activities such as job schedules and backups; and take corrective actions if needed.

D2C monitors the service quality over several quality aspects (performance, availability, capacity, security) from a business perspective. If needed, it takes action to restore service levels. This includes activities and processes such as:
- End-user support (using self-help/self-service and service desk)
- Service monitoring and event management
- Incident management
- Problem management
- Operations management activities such as job scheduling, housekeeping, etc.
- Service-level management

A number of scenarios can be used to evaluate how the IT organization is currently supporting this value stream. This analysis should identify:
- The end-to-end workflow from detecting an exception to actual resolution.
- IT management tools involved in each of these end-to-end flows.
- The data that is managed (and where these are mastered); for example, event, incident, and knowledge records.
- Diagnostics tools to analyze machine data and logs.
- Identify ownership of the processes, data, and tools involved in this value stream.
- Activities in place to prevent service disruptions (and prevent recurring incidents).

Examples of scenarios that can be used for this analysis:

- Unavailability (or outage) of an IT service is detected; follow the workflow for detection to resolution identifying all necessary actions to restore the service (and reduce the impact) including communication with stakeholders.
- Security-related event or vulnerability has been detected; and take actions to mitigate and resolve this event (for example, resolved through a patch/fix).
- Potential performance or capacity-related issues are detected; and take actions such as modify IT resource allocation and resolve performance bottlenecks.
- Unauthorized change in a configuration setting is detected (or new software installed).
- Continuously tune and adjust the IT resource allocation (for example, what policies are available to perform auto-scaling or adjust resources allocated to IT services).
- Execute and monitor job schedules (and other schedules such as backup) according to plans.
- Unauthorized usage of an IT service, application, or other IT asset; identify issue and take appropriate actions.

Examples of activities to be performed in case of a detected alarm/exception by a monitoring tool:

- Detect exception and raise alert (or event).
- Collect events from different monitoring tools.
- Correlate and filter alerts/events.
- Enrich alert/event with other information.
- Determine service and business impact (for example, the service model in the CMDB).
- Perform root cause analysis.
- Initiate automated recovery actions.
- Automatically create an incident (and assign to responsible team).
- Perform incident analysis and diagnosis.
- Notify and inform stakeholders (and keep stakeholders informed).
- Search knowledge base for known errors and work around.
- Assign incident to responsible service providers/third parties.
- Implement temporary fix or resolution; this can include a broad range of measures such as modify resource allocation (capacity).
- Initiate emergency change (if appropriate).
- Close incident and related alerts/events.

Typical gaps identified for this D2C value stream in some IT organizations:

- Lacking sufficient monitoring capabilities (dependent upon end-users reporting exceptions). Most services are not monitored.
- No integrated view on the actual status of IT services from a business perspective (consolidating all events and incidents) (service dashboard).
- Long lead time to perform root cause analysis; information is missing to support the diagnosis; difficult to identify responsible provider (resulting in a lot of discussion and re-assignments).
- Lacking self-service capabilities for reporting incidents.
- Lacking self-help capabilities for end-users to find resolutions.
- Lacking structural effort in identifying problems to prevent incidents from recurring (structurally improve IT service delivery).
- Incidents caused by incorrectly applied changes or newly introduced releases (for example, defects not identified during testing).
- Performance-related incidents/problems which cannot be easily analyzed and/or resolved.
- CMDB is lacking insight in service topology or service model (no clear dependencies between CIs).
- Inefficient communication and collaboration between stakeholders (due to incident and problem management activities).
- Over-capacity of IT resources (unused servers, databases, etc.) in one area and under-capacity in other areas (high cost and low performance).
- Manual activities to respond to incidents.
- Unclear ownership and related support teams (or service provider) for each CI or IT service.
- No automation in service recovery remediation.
- Separate procedures to handle security-related incidents (instead of having one process and tool to manage all incidents).
- No easy access to D2C performance metrics and trends to support decision-making (provide insight in the actual performance of supporting activities).

5.2.3   Define IT4IT Ownership and Governance Model

This section describes the key aspects to be covered in the governance model for an IT4IT deployment (where such a deployment includes all the required IT management capabilities consisting of processes, tools, and data). As described in the introduction of this chapter, it is vital to set up a governance model of how IT management capabilities are developed and offered to the IT organization and its business. This section provides high-level guidance which is not part of the formal IT4IT Reference Architecture, and each organization needs to find its own appropriate governance model.

Figure 28 illustrates how the IT4IT capability fits into the overall IT function.

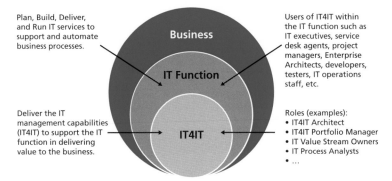

Plan, Build, Deliver, and Run IT services to support and automate business processes.

Users of IT4IT within the IT function such as IT executives, service desk agents, project managers, Enterprise Architects, developers, testers, IT operations staff, etc.

Deliver the IT management capabilities (IT4IT) to support the IT function in delivering value to the business.

Roles (examples):
• IT4IT Architect
• IT4IT Portfolio Manager
• IT Value Stream Owners
• IT Process Analysts
• …

Figure 28: IT4IT Enabling the IT Function to Deliver IT Services to the Business

The business uses IT services as provided by the IT function (brokering and integrating services from many different external sourcing partners such as cloud vendors). These IT services such as an ERP or CRM system need to be development, deployed, and managed by the IT organization (or preferably sourced using standard market services). The IT employees within the IT organization use IT management tools to support their day-to-day tasks such as development tasks, testing tasks, deployment tasks, and support tasks. All these standard tools (referred to as IT4IT applications or solutions) used by the IT function itself can be provided by an "IT4IT organization" (which can be a virtual organization).

An IT4IT governance model must be set up in order to encourage desirable behavior in development and maintenance of these IT management practices and IT management applications (and required metrics/KPIs, skills, roles, processes, and procedures). It should reach across organizational boundaries by setting up a simple decision and review structure. It specifies a decision-making authority at different levels in the organization governing the lifecycle of the IT4IT applications. The structure should be kept simple and effective so that all decisions related to the roll-out and maintenance of IT4IT capabilities are in line with the IT strategy and support the IT management strategic direction.

A number of key roles (or positions) within the IT organization need to be
defined for managing the IT management processes and tools needed to support
the IT4IT value streams.

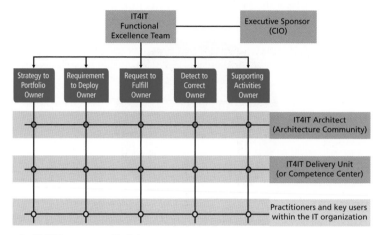

Figure 29: An IT4IT Governance Model

Figure 29 shows the key roles that need to be assigned within the IT function.
The idea is to create a Functional Excellence (FE) team focusing on all the
capabilities and practices needed to run the business of IT. This team ensures
that each value stream is optimally designed to support the IT employees
in doing their day-to-day work; and automate the IT processes as much as
economically possible. The formal ownership of all IT processes and data
definitions is part of this team as well. The FE team is representing the "demand"
role for IT4IT automation capabilities to be delivered by the IT4IT Delivery
Unit. An IT4IT architect needs to be appointed (with potentially additional
architects and tool specialists covering specific expertise areas such as security
and information risk management) working within the overall architecture
function of the IT organization, to ensure alignment with overall IT architecture
and roadmaps (such as technology direction).

For each value stream a focal point, leader, or owner needs be assigned who is
part of the overall IT4IT FE team.

It is also important to identify an executive sponsor such as the CIO for the
overall IT4IT capability.

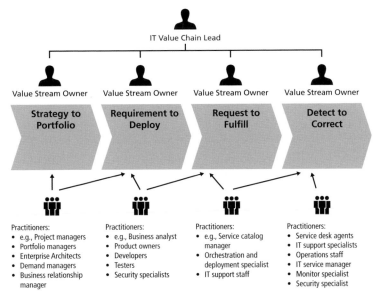

Figure 30: IT Value Stream Owners

The value stream owners stay in close contact with the key stakeholders (or practitioners) involved in the actual execution of the IT management activities such as project managers, developers, testers, support specialists, operations staff, security specialists, etc. The value stream owners are not directly involved in day-to-day delivery of services to the business – but define the standard practices of how the work should be managed. The IT specialists executing day-to-day management activities provide important input to improve these practices; they also need to be empowered to influence how the work should be performed. These IT specialists use the tools as provided by the IT4IT Delivery Unit using practices and standards as agreed with the value stream owners. It is therefore essential that the value stream owners are in close contact with the key practice leads across the different IT teams to capture feedback and adjust the standard practices accordingly.

For the development and support of IT4IT solutions (IT management applications or tools), a portfolio manager is assigned managing the entire application portfolio needed to run IT. The IT4IT portfolio includes applications such as an Enterprise Architecture (EA) system, Project Portfolio Management (PPM) system, test management tools, monitoring tools, event management system, IT service desk or ITSM system, and CMDB.

It would be good to set up a competence center with all required skills and expertise to deliver the IT management tools (a kind of DevOps team for IT management applications). This competence center preferably uses standard software packages (such as delivered through SaaS) supporting the IT4IT value streams and IT4IT related standards and best practices.

In this governance model the IT4IT architect, IT4IT portfolio manager, value stream owners, and executive sponsor have an essential role as main steering committee for IT4IT related decisions. In addition, it is also important to build a complete list of all key stakeholders within the IT management domain. This covers all stakeholders such as process owners, IT executives, IT managers, architects, senior users, IT management tool specialists, security specialists, and so on.

The IT4IT organization
There are several examples of IT organizations, such as at Shell (see Appendix A), that have implemented a dedicated delivery unit (or competence center) with a focus on IT4IT capabilities. This department is responsible for the development, maintenance, and support of the IT management solutions. It acts as internal IT service provider providing IT4IT capabilities as a service using the overall IT4IT Reference Architecture as guidance.

5.2.3.1 IT4IT Value Stream Owner

For each IT4IT value stream, a practice owner needs to be assigned. This person is responsible for all capabilities and practices within the value stream. This covers ownership of the IT processes, IT data definitions, and functional components. This person needs to have a good understanding of the IT4IT standard, ITIL, the TOGAF standard, PMBOK, COBIT, SCRUM, and other practices relevant for each value stream.

In the governance model the value stream owners are in close contact with the "users" of IT management solutions – specifically senior IT employees and/or key IT specialists. The value stream owner discusses current and target IT management capabilities with these key stakeholders and practitioners throughout the IT organization.

Activities to be performed by the value stream owner include the following:
- Design the overall value stream in terms of capabilities, processes, data, and integrations; in close collaboration with the IT4IT architects.
- Develop value stream best practices, processes, and standards.
- Develop work instructions and guidelines.
- Define requirements for IT4IT tooling (to support the functional components).
- Define key metrics and KPIs to be managed.
- Define roles and responsibilities within each value stream and IT process.
- Define data needs (and data quality requirements).
- Define required skills and competences; and define the required training needed to perform specific functions.
- Perform evaluation and assessment of current practices; collect feedback from IT specialists to continuously improve the IT management capabilities.
- Define priorities for improvements and new initiatives.
- Perform market research to understand trends and new IT management practices (and standards).

Additional resources can be assigned to the value stream owners to provide additional support such as ITIL process consultants, process managers, and other practice specialists (for example, test management specialist, cloud automation specialist, and so on). This team develops the standard best practices and continuously improves the capabilities for managing IT.

Key deliverables created by the value stream owners are:
- Standard IT processes, procedures, and guidelines (and defined best practices)
- Agreed KPIs and metrics; and measurement practices
- Assessments of current maturity of functions/processes within the value streams
- Value stream improvement plans
- Data definitions (of the IT4IT standard data model) to ensure consistency between data sources and standard naming conventions are used
- Captured demands and requirements for new or modified IT4IT tools
- Training plans

5.2.3.2   IT4IT Architect (or IT4IT Segment Architect)

The IT4IT architect, part of the Enterprise Architecture community, is overall accountable to design an IT4IT architecture and high-level design to cover all required IT management capabilities from an end-to-end perspective.

The IT4IT architect defines and manages the overall IT management architecture in close collaboration with the value stream owners. This team can consist of multiple architects:
- IT4IT segment architect
- IT4IT process architect (supporting the value stream owners in design processes)
- IT4IT solution architect
- IT4IT security architect
- IT4IT data architect

The IT4IT architect

It is essential to assign one IT4IT lead architect responsible for the IT4IT domain. The IT4IT architect is responsible for defining the target architecture of managing the business of IT, working with the different stakeholders to build a coherent and integrated model for managing IT.

A solution architect is involved in the architecture and high-level design of IT4IT solutions (or IT management tools/applications) together with the IT4IT portfolio manager and competence center responsible for the development and maintenance of these IT4IT solutions. The IT4IT portfolio manager governs the development and operations of the IT4IT applications within the portfolio.

Key outputs:
- IT4IT segment architecture (current and target blueprint)
- Solution architecture (per IT management solution/tool)
- Agreed common data model (with clear data definitions and ownership)
- High-level design of solutions and integrations with external vendors
- Perform market research of IT management standards, practices, and tools
- Discuss IT management trends and tool alternatives with analysts in this area
- Participate in IT management tool selection; recommended IT management tools and required integrations
- IT process architecture

- Standards and policies related to IT management tools (such as using REST APIs, conformance to IT4IT standards, support for SAML)

The IT4IT architect also stays in close contact with tool vendors to discuss roadmaps, new features, new releases, and so on.

5.2.3.3 IT4IT Portfolio Manager (or IT4IT Manager)

It is important to manage IT management processes and tools as a single portfolio similar to other IT portfolios. Therefore, each IT organization should assign a portfolio manager for IT4IT services. This manager manages all IT management solutions used within the IT organization. This person is responsible for overseeing the complete landscape and solutions available to support the IT function.

Example: development teams using their own tools

The IT organization often has defined a number of standard solutions for managing software development. This consists of a tool-chain (or pipeline) of development and test management tools, covering requirements management, IDE, source code management, and so on. However, typically different teams have implemented their own tools and practices because they believe their own tools are better or they want to control their own practices. As a result, each team is managing their own tools and procedures and not leveraging integration with other teams.

Often each team have developed their own reporting tools, utilized third-party document management/collaboration, or used other databases to fill-in the gaps of existing tools and processes.

Preferably IT specialists such as developers and testers can fully focus on delivering new releases and value to the business and not developing or maintaining IT management tools. The goal of the IT4IT approach is to enable the IT specialists to do their work more effectively and efficiently by providing a standard, integrated, and lean IT management toolkit with preconfigured best practices. The IT specialists can focus on doing their job for the business without having to build and maintain their own set of tools.

The IT4IT portfolio manager is responsible for ensuring the entire IT4IT portfolio is managed in alignment with defined roadmaps, required investments, and necessary upgrades. In addition, the portfolio manager is responsible for analyzing the cost and performance of the portfolio – and discussing portfolio rationalization opportunities with the IT4IT architect and value stream owners.

5.2.3.4 IT4IT Delivery Unit (Competence Center)

This organization is responsible for the actual design, development, test, deployment, and operations of IT4IT management tools. This team (or teams) configures the IT4IT tools and builds the required integrations. This team has the skills and competences related to configuring, integrating, and operating the new IT management toolkit.

The IT4IT delivery unit delivers an integrated IT management system (combining multiple tools from different vendors) as a service to the IT organization. It leverages standard offerings from the market (for example, SaaS) provided by the various IT management solutions vendors as well as open source products.

This team consists of a number of roles and specialists including:
- Business analysts to discuss requirements with value stream owners
- IT management tool specialists
- Integration specialists (of building integration between tools and external service providers)
- IT management support specialists

Activities to be performed by the IT4IT competence center include:
- Participate in tool selections.
- Design and configure IT management tools.
- Build and maintain interfaces between tools and suppliers (preferably just configure not customize).
- Build standard IT management reports and scorecards (leverage standard IT4IT metrics/KPIs).
- Perform daily support of IT management tools.
- Engage with IT management software vendors (for example, for operations and support).

More often these IT management tools are delivered as SaaS services. However, these new and modern IT management tools also require new skills and expertise to configure and use these solutions. Examples of new expertise and skills needed in this team include:

- Cloud automation specialists (how to build and configure cloud automation capabilities)
- Operations data analytics
- Service catalog specialists
- Orchestration and run book automation specialists (build orchestration workflows and integrations with technology-specific tools or platforms)
- Continuous delivery tool-chain specialist (how to build an Continuous Delivery pipeline)
- Monitoring specialists (for example, for business process monitoring and application performance monitoring)
- Test automation specialists

5.2.4 Define IT Management Vision, Mission, and Strategy

Before the IT4IT architecture is defined in more detail, it is important to define the overall mission and vision of the IT organization and its required IT management capabilities. The IT strategy and plans for the IT function drive the vision and mission of the IT4IT capability. In addition, it is important to investigate the medium and long-term technology roadmap.

The IT strategy, IT vision, and technology plans provide the key themes as input to the IT management vision.

Key input from the IT strategy and technology architecture for the IT4IT vision and strategy includes:

- New business plans and direction
- IT becoming a service broker (and integrator)
- New goals for the IT organization, such as to reduce cost and improve cost transparency
- New sourcing strategies (outsource or insource)
- Move applications to the cloud (such as SaaS) or building a hybrid cloud environment (using, for example, PaaS platforms)
- Use new technology concepts such as converged infrastructure or Software-Defined Data Center
- HR strategy for IT (including new skills and competences)

- Target direction of the enterprise standard technologies; including new strategic IT technology vendors (such as virtualization technology, storage, network, and so on)

IT technology plan

A key input to the IT4IT roadmap is the expected changes in the IT technology landscape. These new technologies can have a big impact on the IT4IT management model.

How will the technology landscape change over time? What is the target technology architecture (and defined standards)? For example, new technologies or delivery methods such as:
- Cloud (such as IaaS, PaaS, and SaaS)
- Big data
- Mobile app development
- Converged infrastructure
- Open source platforms
- New deployment methods, such as using containers (for example, Docker)
- Infrastructure as code
- Service-Oriented Architecture (SOA) (and service components)
- Software-Defined Network (SDN) or Software-Defined anything
- New software development languages/methods
- API-driven ecosystem
- Internet of Things (IoT)

It is important to understand the overall strategy of technologies and vendors in the technology stack as each of these key technologies come with their own IT management tools and capabilities; for example, SAP management tools (for SAP), Microsoft tools for Windows, VMware for the VMware stack, and so on. Cloud vendors such as Microsoft Windows Azure and Amazon also provide their own IT management tools and APIs which need to be integrated into the overall IT4IT landscape.

The introduction of new technologies or new IT delivery models requires thinking about how this new technology will be managed. An IT organization that is planning to move a significant number of applications to the cloud (IaaS or SaaS) requires the development of new cloud management capabilities, such as:

- Self-service portal and catalog management
- Cloud brokering services (manage cloud catalog)
- Cloud provisioning services including support for provisioned services
- Cloud monitoring
- Cloud consumption and cost management services (in combination with monitoring services)
- Cloud security and risk management
- License management (for software running on cloud environments)

Typically, the impact of introducing new services to the IT management capabilities is not covered very well in transformation programs.

New paradigms

Example of new paradigms and concepts for the new IT organization:

- Manage IT as a business (including an economic view)
- IT4IT value stream approach
- Continuous improvement as part of the DNA of the organization
- Lean Kanban
- Continuous Delivery
- Lean and Agile practices
- Bimodal IT
- DevOps
- NoOps
- Empowerment of IT teams
- Instrument applications during development (for operations)
- Secure by design (ensure secure systems during development)
- Automation of IT activities
- Design thinking
- Holacracy (self-organization)
- Service brokering, deliver everything as a service (IT as a service)
- ...

It is already mentioned that IT management is not just about operational support of delivered services. It is responsible for the end-to-end service value chain, from conceptual service to actual deployed CIs. IT management needs a vision to manage the IT in this perspective, taking these new paradigms into account. The IT management vision and mission can be documented (for example, using a business canvas model) answering questions such as:

- What is IT management? Why is IT management becoming more important? And why is it so difficult?
- How will the IT landscape change in the coming years (for example, cloud services) and how should IT management respond to this?
- What is the value of IT for the business?
- How do we manage IT today? And how should we want to manage IT in the future?
- What are the key imperatives for the new IT organization?
- What are the most important problems and issues?
- What new skills and competences are needed to manage this new IT?
- What new IT management capabilities are needed (for example, self-service and more automation of IT tasks)?

5.2.5   Define the Target IT4IT Architecture

One of key issues of the current way of working within the IT organization is that historically IT processes and tools have been implemented without a long-term vision (without the equivalent of a city plan), but rather the outcome of many *ad hoc* decisions and isolated tool implementations. This has resulted in a complex IT management process and tooling landscape. It becomes, however, more and more important to define a target blueprint of how IT services need to be managed. This new blueprint needs, for example, to describe how the new IT organization can manage a multi-vendor IT ecosystem including the IaaS, PaaS, and SaaS providers.

This target IT4IT architecture is using the IT4IT Reference Architecture as the blueprint. This architecture describes the Future Mode of Operation (FMO) covering all IT4IT capabilities comprising of processes, data, application functionality, and interfaces. The target architecture should also address the required skills and new roles in the IT organization.

Key inputs to the creation of the target IT4IT architecture are:

- Business strategy and plans
- IT strategy
- IT management strategy and vision (from the previous step)
- New technology standards and roadmap; and strategic technology vendors (such as hybrid-cloud, SaaS) – leveraging new technology platforms or

technologies such as containers or micro-services will directly impact the required IT4IT related management capabilities
- Cloud strategy
- Sourcing strategy
- The IT4IT Reference Architecture (Levels 1 to 3)
- Other relevant standards and best practices, such as ITIL and COBIT
- Various tool vendor reference architectures (Level 4)
- Relevant best practices and standards providing requirements and specifications for specific areas such as PMBOK for project management, SCRUM for agile development, the TOGAF standard for Enterprise Architecture, and ITIL for ITSM
- IT4IT baseline assessment results (and value stream analysis)

It is also recommended to use the TOGAF Architecture Development Method (ADM) in the design and realization of the target architecture.

The IT4IT Reference Architecture provides the overall blueprint for this IT4IT target architecture, on which the company specifics are added, such as:
- Defining the current and target portfolio of IT management applications
- Mapping of target IT management tools (and integrations) to the IT4IT Reference Architecture
- Mapping of selected other best practices and standards, such as ITIL and PMBOK
- Information/data model mapped to IT management tools

As part of defining the target state IT operating model and IT4IT architecture, the new skills and competences need to be identified, such as illustrated in Figure 31.

5.2.6 Perform Gap Analysis
In the next step of the transformation, the gap analysis is performed. The gaps between the target model and the current model are identified. This gap analysis uses the specifications of the IT4IT Reference Architecture as the overarching blueprint. This blueprint identifies all requirement functional components, data entities, and integrations. The gap analysis should look at all required ingredients of the target IT operating model, such as:
- Organization, roles, and responsibilities
- Skills and competences

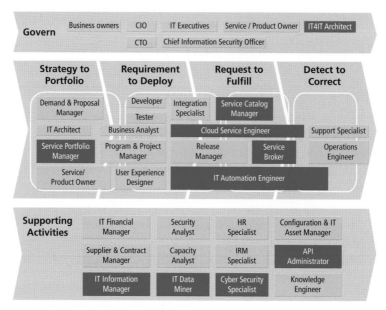

Figure 31: Examples of New Roles Within the IT Function

- Information/data model (verify data mastership, ownership, data quality, etc.)
- Processes and procedures
- IT management tools (and integrations)
- Delivery and support model related to IT management practices and tools

The gap analysis must be validated with different key stakeholders. The exercise can be performed for individual functional components, value streams, or the entire IT Value Chain. There are different approaches for performing this gap analysis. Examples of techniques which can be used include:

- Perform "as-is" *versus* "to-be" analysis using two sets of architecture viewpoints, based on the functional components as defined the IT4IT Reference Architecture. This first viewpoint is the "as-is" or current situation, the second is the "to-be" or target situation. By making an overlay of the two viewpoints, the gap can be made visual for decision-makers.
- Another technique is to use a heat-map based on the functional component models per value stream, to identify using three colors (red, orange, and green) how good the fit-gap result is (green being a good fit, red a gap, and orange some work to do to achieve a fit). This can provide key decision-makers with an easy-to-understand visualization of the "as-is" state.

- Conduct application portfolio analysis related to IT management tools, plotting applications onto one number of matrix diagrams covering a number of x-axis and y-axis scores such as "business fit" (or business value), "costs", "risks (for example, end-of-life), and "architectural fit", which can be used to identify portfolio rationalization opportunities.

Key activities to perform in the gap analysis are:
- Determine and assess the "as-is" situation (as described in previous sections).
- Determine the "to-be" operating model illustrated by a number of use-cases (or scenarios).
  Example use-cases to describe the "to-be" situation include:
  - Strategy to Portfolio: Manage the portfolio of services and investments; for example, how to handle the funnel of demands and prioritize investments.
  - Requirement to Deploy: Manage the end-to-end workflow from a new requirement to actual release into production, covering the automated build, test, and deployment.
  - Request to Fulfill: Fully automated self-service provisioning of requests; end-users requesting services from a service portal from initiation through fulfillment, updating the CMDB, monitoring consumption and costs.
  - Detect to Correct: More advanced monitoring of IT services; e.g., using service alarms prior to outages. Monitoring and automation use-cases; proactive monitoring, run book automation for automatic service recovery, etc.
  - Detect to Correct: Building service models for the actual service CIs that incorporate SLA and OLA dependencies, so impact analysis in the change, event, incident, and problem functional components can be improved.
- Perform gap analysis for the current against the to-be situation using the different use-cases and scenarios.
- Take action on the identified gaps with stakeholders; e.g., define IT4IT portfolio rationalization opportunities (e.g., decommission applications).

During the analysis different type of gaps will be identified, for example:
- Missing skills and competences related to the IT4IT approach (for example, automation of IT tasks).
- Lacking specific capabilities such as self-service enablement, automated deployment, application performance monitoring, IT service analytics and reporting, test automation, security monitoring, operations data analytics, and so on.

- Lacking agreed standard solutions for specific functional components such as an integrated PPM system, ITSM system, or CMDB.
- Multiple tools supporting the same functional component such as multiple project management tools (which could be rationalized).
- Identify rationalization and consolidation opportunities to reduce the complexity of the IT4IT tooling landscape.
- Identify IT management tools, which are candidates for retirement (or need to be upgraded).
- Identify homegrown IT management tools that could be replaced by market solutions.
- Missing interfaces between processes and tools to share data.
- Data gaps such as lacking formal trusted system or master data sources for the data entities identified in the IT4IT Reference Architecture.
- Pinpointed functional components without sufficient support of best practices, tools, and data.
- Identify IT management tools with a high level of customizations.
- Highlight functional components with multiple solutions that lack integrations, lack a common data model, have overlapping functionality, etc.
- Identify opportunities to automate manual IT management tasks.
- Lacking IT management tool governance and ownership.

Table 4 provides a number of typical gaps or issues found in many IT organizations grouped by IT4IT value stream related to IT management capabilities.

Table 4: Typical Gaps/Issues Grouped by IT4IT Value Stream

Value Stream	Example of Gaps
Strategy to Portfolio	• No consolidated portfolio of all IT services and applications (single system of record). • No integration between service portfolio and CMDB. • Lacking periodic service portfolio reviews and creation of service/application roadmaps. • No single funnel to manage all demands and proposals. • Data quality issues related to Enterprise Architecture, service portfolio, and project portfolio data. • No enterprise standard PPM process and tool. • No linked project portfolio and service portfolio. • No insight in actual value, performance, costs, and risks per service/application.

Value Stream	Example of Gaps
	• No process and system to manage the portfolio backlog. • Lacking standard IT investment prioritizing capabilities. • No insight in technology debt (missing analysis of end-of-life/support of key technologies). • No integration of service portfolio with the IT GRC management system (for example, to perform a Business Impact Assessment (BIA)).
Requirement to Deploy	• No integrated system to manage requirements, development tasks, and test cases. • Requirements and development activities managed using spreadsheets. • Different practices and tools to support agile software development (no common agreed model for different delivery chains). • No traceability from requirement, development, test, to release. • Limited use of automated testing due to lacking test automation capabilities (mainly manual testing). • No standard process and system for application release automation. • No standard Continuous Delivery tool-chain.
Request to Fulfill	• No consolidated service catalog covering all services provided by the IT organization. • Many different security management tools not integrated into the overall IT4IT landscape. • No standard self-service portal for handling all types of requests. • No central administration managing all user access rights and subscriptions to applications and IT services (lacking a subscription administration). • Mainly manual deployment and provisioning activities (limited automation). • Lacking monitoring of actual usage of services. • No chargeback or showback of actual usage to consumers.

Value Stream	Example of Gaps
Detect to Correct	• Lacking service monitoring strategy and vision (many different fragmented monitoring tools). • No consolidated event management system (for event correlation and impact assessment). • Mainly infrastructure monitoring. Limited number of applications monitored from a business perspective. • No standard application performance monitoring solution. • Limited self-help for end-users. • No proactive problem management. • No operations analytics tools (for example, to identify trends).
Supporting Activities	• No insight in costs of IT services and applications based on actual consumption (having a consolidated IT financial management system). • No standard IT data warehouse or reporting system; lacking standard IT service reporting with agreed metrics and KPIs. • Contract management not integrated with CMDB and other IT management systems. • Lacking capabilities to perform invoice verification (related to actual consumption and performed activities of vendors). • Lot a manual effort to create periodic reports. • No single system of record for all IT risks and compliance issues (IT GRC system).

5.2.7   Define the IT4IT Roadmap and Build the Business Case

Although the IT4IT transformation is fluid and influenced by variation and emotion, a plan is required. The approach is to produce a roadmap of change working with all the relevant stakeholders to ensure the plan is seen as a joint effort. The gap analysis has identified a number of major initiatives and improvements that need to be implemented. After the gap analysis, a high-level roadmap and IT4IT portfolio plan needs to be constructed. Potentially there are a number of quick-wins, which can be implemented sooner – such as consolidation, and rationalization of some IT management applications.

Based upon the gap analysis and discussion with the different stakeholders a large number of potential initiatives needed improve the IT management capabilities can be identified. A complete list of these candidates needs to be compiled into one overall funnel and portfolio backlog. Examples of potential initiatives or improvement opportunities are:

- Build an integrated service and application portfolio management capability (process and tool).
- Improve service monitoring (proactive monitoring) and automated response to alerts.
- Implement Continuous Delivery practice and tool-chain (covering build, test, and deployment automation).
- Implement Lean and Agile development methods (such as using SCRUM).
- Standardize application release automation.
- CMDB data quality improvements (such as using discovery and service modeling).
- Improve integrations with external service providers (for example, ticketing/ case exchange).
- Implement test management system and test automation (and test data management).
- IT cost showback/chargeback.
- Set up an IAM solution (for managing user identities and access rights).
- Replace or upgrade existing IT management tools (for example, when they are end-of-life).
- Implement a central self-service portal with an integrated service catalog.
- Implement (or improve) software asset management (and license compliance reporting).
- Cloud management capability (for example, cloud management platform).

It is important that all these initiatives are managed within a single portfolio and a single funnel (by the IT4IT capability). This facilitates the creation of a consolidated roadmap for all these IT management capabilities to ensure alignment with the overall IT management vision and direction.

To organize and categorize all these different IT4IT related initiatives the following methods can be used:

- Group initiatives per IT4IT value stream (with the identified value stream owner).
- Identify key themes and business epics used to create the roadmap and link initiatives to these high-level themes.
- Use capability-based planning or scenario-based planning techniques.

An example of a method to create and visualize the IT4IT roadmap is shown in Figure 32.

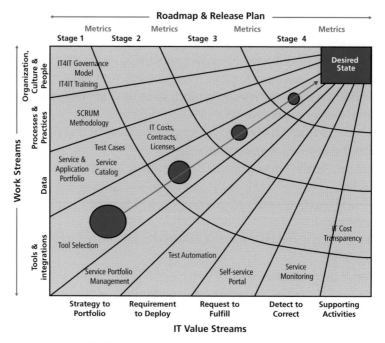

Figure 32: Example of an IT4IT Roadmap Visualization

Key activities to define the roadmap and business case are:
- Define the IT4IT program:
  - Set up governance, corporate alignment, management, integration in the IT department, program budgets, and target resources for the program.
- Define the overall IT4IT roadmap (aligned with the target IT4IT architecture):
  - Identify and agree the functional components and products that are in focus (scope and boundary statement), the critical systems, technology drivers, and timelines.
  - Identify the strategic themes and create a holistic IT4IT portfolio backlog (identifying all proposed initiatives and investment opportunities).
- Define the quick-wins in the program:
  - Identify the low-hanging fruits in the roadmap; they may realize pilots.

- Define the investments and business case:
  - Build the business case: Link the key initiative to the overall drivers or objectives of the business. Gain support from senior business leaders and senior stakeholders. Set a baseline for assessing the impact of the investigation. Estimate costs and resource requirements.
  - Assess readiness: Identify the budgetary, staffing, technology, and other requirements necessary to prepare the business for the investigation. Develop a total cost of ownership analysis framework. Review established policies for assessing risk and managing governance.
  - Pilot or prototype: Identify a group to pilot, or develop a prototype for the investigation. Develop and communicate detailed requirements. Manage the pilot/prototype. Assess and communicate the results.
  - Gain approval: Analyze findings of the readiness assessment and pilot or prototype effort, and revise the strategy and business case accordingly. Present findings of the investigation to senior stakeholders and business leaders.

One of the biggest challenges is getting the required support (and funding) for adopting the IT4IT Reference Architecture and associated roadmap within the different levels of the IT organization. Once stakeholders support the vision and approach, the next challenge is to obtain approval for the required IT budget to fund the different initiatives needed to implement an integrated IT4IT system landscape including the transformation cost of acquiring and training new skills and competences. Usually a business case needs to be produced to receive funding for the proposed initiatives (and making the identified benefits measurable). In some cases this IT4IT improvement program can be embedded in a larger technology transformation initiative; for example, when an organization is making significant investments in migrating to a cloud operating model or is involved in a larger outsourcing initiative. It is essential that, when these kind of significant changes are introduced, there is funding reserved for the implementation of the new IT management capabilities. For example, when the organization is planning to migrate a large number of applications to the cloud – there is an opportunity to treat this as a greenfield implementation, safeguarding the required funding the build the new IT management framework.

5.2.8   Set Up an IT4IT Model Office

A sound parallel activity during the design of the target state and during the execution of the IT4IT roadmap is to set up an "IT4IT model office" to demonstrate the new way of working. A model office is a controlled environment where IT staff and stakeholders can experience the benefits of an integrated approach to IT management (a kind of IT4IT experience center). This environment can also be used as a development and test environment for IT4IT capabilities. To provide real value it should be implemented within the IT organization with a representative standard technology stack such as the standard internal hosting platforms, storage, network technologies, and also links to the external cloud for automated provisioning.

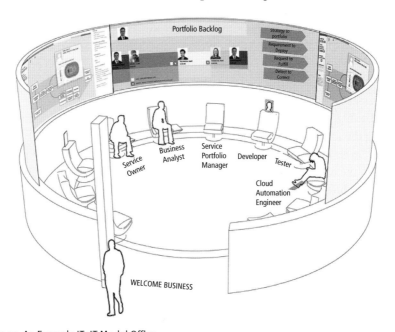

Figure 33: An Example IT4IT Model Office

The model office is used for a number of purposes, including:
- Obtain stakeholder buy-in to support the new IT operation model (tell and sell); demonstrate the new way of working.
- Get active participation and involvement of key stakeholders, decision-makers, and practice leads (at earlier stages).
- Provide room for experimentation and exploration of new ideas, learning by doing.

- Build and demonstrate the vision of the new IT operating model.
- Prototype of the end-to-end workflows across the value streams (using use-cases) to determine most appropriate set-up for the IT function.
- Validate the overall IT4IT architecture with working products (from different vendors) that can be integrated.
- Perform tool selections with a selected number of IT management tool vendors (and ensure fit into the overall IT management landscape).
- Confirm the feasibility and business case (for example, show how manual activities can be automated).
- Provide the high-level designs as input for the actual implementation (input to the portfolio backlog for the IT4IT capability).
- Validate the new way of working with the different stakeholders (combining process, tool, new roles, and data perspectives).
- Design and validate IT automation patterns (for example, automated provisioning).
- Validate, test, and verify how new technologies (such as cloud or converged infrastructure) can be managed.
- Configure and test integrations with external service providers and standard APIs and tools part of specific technology stacks (as each cloud vendor or technology vendor provides its own management APIs and tools).
- Provide a vehicle for experimentation with new IT management concepts and practices.

The model office demonstrates how the new IT function will operate. This is where all aspects of the implementation will be exposed in an integrated manner. It comprises modeling for the business, functional, technical, and implementation model. Modeling for the implementation model ensures proper data integration between components and addresses the suitable functionality for the technical model. The model office is recommended to adopt a DevOps set-up, so it can deliver outcomes rapidly. It applies Agile and Lean development practices, and works on a number of iterations and releases based upon a prioritized IT4IT portfolio backlog. Different scenarios and alternatives can be prototyped and evaluated before the actual decision of buying IT management tools is taken.

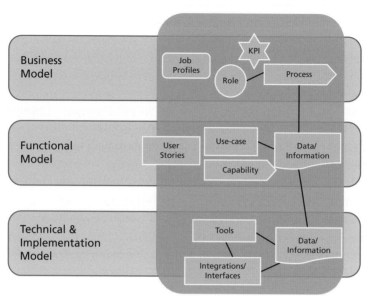

Figure 34: IT4IT Model Office Modeling Layers

A model office can have a physical format, where all model office members are in the same room, but it can also be a virtual team. The team members will select the use-cases based on the program backlog. It is important to keep track of the decisions made, as these will be required for design and build in a later stage. It is also essential to have a representative IT technology stack which can be used to execute the use-cases such as the provisioning of cloud resources and deployment of applications.

Use-cases are used in the model office to guide the modeling of end-to-end workflows, in order to validate a number of proof points. Proof points can be made on either layer of the model (business, functional, technical, implementation); they define, for example, the correct integration between systems, relationships between artifacts or data objects, and the business support of the case as a whole. Proof points will have a thesis and substantiation.

Use-cases can cover the entire IT Value Chain, or focus on one or more value streams. Examples of use-cases are: raise demand for a new service, enhancement request (new requirement) for an existing service, request access to a business application, or retire an existing service. These use-cases may seem small, but they typically cover a broad range of activities within the entire chain. The model office demonstrates to the organization (to key stakeholders) how these use-cases will be executed in the new IT operating model. The format of this demonstration can be a combination of actual working software, presentations, video capture, or just as simple as a document with flow diagrams and screenshots. Key users (IT specialists and IT support staff) need to be involved to influence and determine how the new IT4IT system will be designed and configured. The model office is an important vehicle to empower key users to be involved in defining the future operation model and to ensure that the new way of working will be adopted by the IT stakeholders.

Around the model office there must be a core team created with motivated and skilled people (linked to key stakeholders within the IT organization), giving them the environment and support they need to accelerate the implementation aligned with the IT4IT vision. The model office increases the likelihood that people within the organization will understand, embrace, and even drive change.

5.2.9 Execute the IT4IT Transformation Roadmap

The execution of the IT4IT transformation roadmap and implementation of the new IT4IT architecture requires a lean, iterative, and agile approach. This transformation is typically a long-term journey in which the current operation model is replaced by a target IT operating model based upon the IT4IT standard.

The IT4IT roadmap delivers the required changes in the IT operating model in a structured and architecture-driven manner aligned with the IT strategy and IT management vision. This implementation encompasses all changes such as new organizational roles, changing behaviors, new skills and competences, process improvements, and tools. This is a fundamentally different approach than how the IT function currently has been implementing IT management capabilities, moving from silo'ed and fragmented initiatives to a coordinated and collaborative team-based approach.

The transformation should use the IT4IT standard itself (and related best practices such as the TOGAF standard and SCRUM), to manage the IT4IT services throughout its lifecycle, for example:
- Strategy to Portfolio: maintain a portfolio of IT4IT applications, create roadmaps, and manage the IT4IT portfolio backlog.

- Requirement to Deploy: use standard practices such as SCRUM to build the release and product backlog; define the different sprints (or iterations) to continuously improve the IT4IT capabilities.

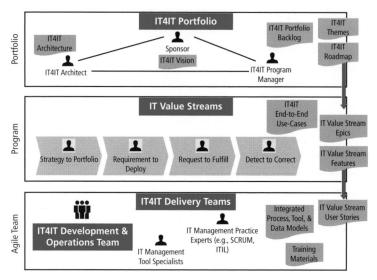

Figure 35: IT4IT Delivery Model

Delivery of the IT4IT transformation requires an integrated portfolio, program, and project management approach, as illustrated in Figure 35, using practices such as SAFe, SCRUM, and other Agile practices. At the portfolio level, the overall governance is performed including investment planning, portfolio backlog, and creating an overall roadmap. The IT4IT architecture is captured here to drive the overall implementation at the program and team levels. At the program level, the different value streams need to be positioned to define and maintain a more detailed value stream backlog covering the features to be developed in the upcoming release planning. The next level contains the different IT4IT delivery teams responsible for delivering IT management solutions in a number of sprints including the related processes and training materials.

Key aspects to be considered as part of the transition roadmap include:
- Implement the IT4IT governance model assigning key roles and responsibilities including the IT4IT architect, the IT4IT portfolio manager, and value stream owners.

- Create an overarching target IT4IT architecture (using the IT4IT Reference Architecture) to guide and steer the overall implementation and roadmap, but also considering that the design emerges during iterations.
- Link the IT4IT initiatives with the overall IT strategy and vision, including the new technology services and sourcing strategy.
- Forming core teams around the value streams headed by the value stream owner to design and prioritize releases (and optimize value streams as a whole).
- Provide clear focus on what needs to be done or improved.
- Decommission non-strategic IT management applications (and prevent further investments).
- Build an IT4IT portfolio of current and target tools including their roadmap.
- Focus on delivery of value around the value streams instead of implementing separate tools or improving individual processes.
- Embed "Management of Change" into the overall program approach.
- Prevent large projects (with long lead times), but rather build incrementally and continuously improve capabilities based upon feedback from users (creating a flow and cadence in the IT organization).
- Prevent customizations and homegrown solutions (but rather select IT management solutions with preconfigured best practices and workflows aligned with the IT4IT standard).
- Consider the art of the possible with the current maturity of IT management tools (which are not always that mature). Vendors often exaggerate their tool capabilities and underestimate the work needed to implement them in the "real world".
- No *ad hoc* tool selections (for specific capabilities), but rather consider the bigger picture within the IT4IT Reference Architecture.
- Use prototyping and use-case modeling in the model office to verify how tools can be integrated and manage the specific technology stack of the organization.
- Upfront training of IT4IT standard and related best practices to ensure all stakeholders and team members share the same terminology and concepts.

The IT4IT Reference Architecture, and in the future supplier certifications, will also help you to select the right IT management applications to implement the required functional components within the architecture.

The implementation of the IT4IT approach will have a significant impact on all people within the IT organization. It provides new ways of working which will affect all people, processes, and technologies such as:

- Automation of tasks previously performed by IT specialists
- Functions or jobs not needed any more (because these are now distributed and embedded into other roles and systems)
- New roles needed, such as a cloud automation engineer maintains automation run books
- New skills and competences needed (but also a new culture)
- Increased transparency of work performed
- Outsourcing of activities to cloud vendors and external service providers

Making users change their behavior is one of the biggest hurdles to the successful deployment of a new IT operating model. However, if correctly executed it will create a new momentum and boost the motivation of IT employees. It results in a new streamlined and agile IT organization, making it attractive for key IT specialists to work in (ability to acquire and retain the right skills and expertise).

Overcome resistance ...
It is a challenging task to create a common vision and target model of how to manage IT. The IT4IT standard aims to deliver an integrated and common blueprint to manage all IT management activities. It provides the concise and structured statement of how to put together a unified IT management system (and shared data) that enables the end-to-end delivery of digital value. This does not necessarily mean one tool framework (or umbrella system) delivered by one tool vendor – but rather a "system" consisting of a collection of inter-connected IT management tools with preconfigured standard best practices and open interfaces.

There will definitively be resistance by different teams and IT specialists. You will get comments such as: we have done this before and it didn't work; this is too complicated; and let IT specialists select their own tools they would like to work with (Bring Your Own Tool (BYOT)).

First, it is good to understand the origin of the fear and resistance of IT specialists (e.g., system administrators, application managers, database managers, network administrators, workplace administrators, and security administrators). To do so we have to look more closely at how specialist IT is currently managed in many IT organizations. Today, specialists have the liberty and authority to purchase and customize specialist tools and point-solutions to support them in their operations. In most cases, these applications are tweaked in such a way that it serves their preferences and at the same time largely, if not completely, automated their operations. So in essence the complete set of tweaked applications have enabled IT specialists to optimize their daily work (however, unfortunately not end-to-end value stream). Thus, replacing the tweaked applications for an integrated IT4IT "system" hits the specialist in two ways. First, their daily work is no longer optimized to conform to their preferences. Second, the integrated IT4IT system may make the IT specialists partly, if not completely, superfluous (for example, using self-service and automated provisioning). Such a direction is particularly hard when you consider the fact that IT specialists are very important for today's IT. As they hold an important position in the reliability and continuity of IT and when all goes south, they are the ones you call at in the middle of the night to solve (major) escalations and to keep your business running. In other words, today's IT specialists are one of the few individuals within your organization who are business-critical. It is for this reason that IT specialists are held in high regard and, as a result, have a great influence on the opinion forming within your organization. The best way to approach such situations is by making IT specialists part of the IT4IT change initiative.

Key additional aspects to be considered for improving the adoption of the IT4IT roadmap are:

- Conduct training and education of all stakeholders related to the IT4IT Reference Architecture (from the start), explaining the new IT operating model.
- Build an IT4IT community of key stakeholders and specialists to create active involvement and participation.
- Promote and communicate the benefits of an IT4IT enabled IT operating model. Effective internal communication is key and requires a plan. Spread the message to IT executives, managers, employees, and outside vendors to gain acceptance and air cover.

- Periodically measure the confidence, perception, and support of key IT stakeholders for the entire IT4IT roadmap (to timely initiate mitigations), and the willingness of people to adopt the new way of working. For any transformation to be successful, resistance to change needs to be measured, understood, and mitigated wherever possible. This includes identifying the disbeliefs at an individual and team level.
- Ensure engagement and involvement of key stakeholders to continuously capture feedback (and recruit ambassadors).
- Develop relevant, real use-cases. Identify what is challenging about the new way of working and have tactics for helping users navigate through the obstacles.
- Pay attention to support and training of the IT management tools. Help users to use the tools and processes in the optimal way (for example, creating internal videos of end-to-end use-cases explaining the how and why).
- Based upon the "as-is" analysis, identify areas where most business value can be achieved (for example, deployment automation of standard technologies using a self-service portal) or automate most frequently performed IT management tasks.
- Identify most suitable areas and teams to perform pilots and enable quick-wins. For example, implement a Continuous Delivery tool-chain (or pipeline) for a specific technology or service team to proof feasibility and learn before these are rolled-out on a large scale.

Appendix A

Case Studies

This chapter describes two case studies about major IT organizations that have chosen to adopt the IT4IT Reference Architecture.

A.1 The Adoption of the IT4IT Standard at Shell

A.1.1 Introduction

Royal Dutch Shell (Shell) is one of the world's largest oil and gas companies having over 94,000 employees in more than 70 countries. The business covers the full spectrum of activities from exploration to retail for oil products and chemicals. The Shell Upstream business explores for and extracts crude oil and natural gas, while the Downstream business refines, supplies, trades, and ships crude worldwide, manufactures and markets a range of products, and produces petrochemicals for industrial customers.

The aspiration of Shell is to be the world's most competitive and innovative energy company. Innovation and technology is a core differentiator for Shell. The IT function needs to support this vision and strategy by providing an optimized portfolio of IT services to support the shifting business demands in a constantly changing business environment. Shell has a large IT function which requires sophisticated and integrated IT management capabilities to ensure IT delivers against expectations while constraining costs and ensuring secure and reliable operations.

A.1.2 Background

Using innovation and technology enables Shell to find more oil, extend the life of production platforms, and enhance profitability by extracting and refining more efficiently. Technology and innovation are also essential to Shell to meet the world's energy demands in a competitive way while building a sustainable energy future. In addition, Shell operates in environments where the most advanced technologies are needed. For example, Shell operates and monitors its oil and gas fields efficiently with SmartFields[3] technology that uses sophisticated sensors for heat and pressure linked to real-time monitoring centers around the world. This allows operators to respond quickly to potential difficulties, optimizing output. Another example is a seismic sensing system using fiber optics to help pinpoint resources more effectively underground. This strong technology bias makes Shell a very intense user of IT.

Some key facts and figures of the Shell IT landscape:

Number of Applications	Over 5,000 business applications
Number of Desktops	140,000+ desktops and laptops in1,800 sites
Number of Servers	25,000 servers
Number of IT Staff	10,000 (including contractors)

There is an increased attention at board level to optimize the value of IT while at the same time reducing IT costs. The former CIO of Shell stated at the launch of The Open Group IT4IT Forum in 2014:

"Like many other companies, Shell faces challenges around matching IT capabilities to core business needs, and reducing IT spend while delivering IT solutions faster. Rapid technological developments like cloud computing, IT consumerization, and big data add further complexity, and we find ourselves in a position where we are increasingly stretched to respond to rising demand and a need for greater agility."

At Shell a number of disruptive IT technologies or ecosystem changes are identified for the near future which require new and integrated IT management capabilities, such as:
- Increasing use of cloud solutions; e.g., SaaS
- Escalating number of devices connected to the network
- Accelerating number of interfaces between applications and external parties
- Increasing volume of changes and releases (due to continuous delivery)
- Increasing security risks; and the need to act more quickly
- Increasing number of external service providers (a more complex IT ecosystem)
- Growing consumption and usage of IT resources (e.g., more transactions, more storage, etc.)

---

3   SmartFields™ is a trademark of Shell International Exploration and Production BV.

This creates a new IT ecosystem in which the Shell IT organization must become more responsive, agile, and cost-effective. As highlighted by Mary Jarrett (IT4IT Manager at Shell) in her presentation at The Open Group launch of the IT4IT Reference Architecture in October 2015:

"IT needs to become quicker, easier to use, perform well every day, and do that at lower cost and risk."

These trends raise the demand for more consolidated and automated IT4IT capabilities. Shell realizes that it must adopt open market standards to provide these integrated capabilities to manage the IT function.

A.1.3   Adoption of the IT4IT Reference Architecture

Because of the lack of applicable standards in the market, Shell has for the last decade developed its own IT management architecture and blueprint to improve and standardize the IT function. This blueprint consisted of a common process model, IT data model, and IT management tool architecture. Best practices such as ITIL, COBIT, SCRUM, and PMBOK were combined to provide a standard delivery model of how to operate IT. However, the implementation of the tools needed to support this IT operating model required a lot of customization and maintenance effort.

During a large outsourcing initiative in 2008, the majority of the IT infrastructure was outsourced to three global external service providers. Shell had to develop its own interfaces to collaborate and integrate with these providers in order to exchange incidents, changes, consumption, and IT costs data – this all due to the lack of open and standard integrations to collaborate with external service providers. There is still a lot of effort involved in the design, configuration, integration, and maintenance of IT management tools. Multiple tools from different vendors are needed to manage the IT estate through its end-to-end lifecycle. Often tools from different vendors (or even from the same vendor) do not integrate well and each vendor has its own proprietary data models, which makes it difficult to share information to improve transparency and support decision-making. Although there are many IT standards and frameworks such as ITIL and COBIT, a major gap remains: each vendor has chosen its own way for how these IT processes are actually performed.

Now the next outsourcing wave is coming in which IT services are moving to the public cloud. As a result, the number of service providers in the IT ecosystem will significantly increase, requiring a different approach for service brokering, integration, and orchestration. With this cloud enablement, a similar challenge as in 2008 is becoming apparent. In this new IT ecosystem automation and integration are becoming even more important, such as automated testing, automated deployment, and provisioning. That is why The Open Group IT4IT Reference Architecture is becoming essential. Instead of continually inventing the wheel itself, Shell engaged with a number of vendors and other organizations to jointly design and develop a standard IT management blueprint. This arrangement paved the way for Shell and several other companies to share their expertise in The Open Group IT4IT Forum.

Shell stands to benefit from this work in various ways – for example, by enabling the vitally needed interoperability in multi-vendor ecosystems and gaining a much deeper insight into what is happening in the IT function – that will highlight opportunities for cost improvement, quality enhancement, and risk reduction.

The IT4IT Reference Architecture is not just a set of documents. As Mary Jarrett stated:
"It is a philosophy which Shell believes in."

This includes, for example:
- Transformation from internal data centers to broker of IT services
- A common data model throughout the lifecycle
- Integrated management capabilities enabling DevOps
- Flexibility for new management models for emerging technologies
- Exchange of information in a growing ecosystem of vendors

Shell believes IT can be delivered faster, better, cheaper, and at lower risk through this holistic IT4IT approach. The IT4IT standard needs to be supported in the IT industry both by IT consumers (such as Shell) and well as service providers and IT management tool vendors.

"We have been working for quite a while, trying to rationalize and build out a portfolio of IT management solutions in Shell – using ITIL and COBIT as process guidance in that space. But it has proven to be quite a difficult journey and we believe that we can only really get value from our investments, and get to the deep and detailed insights we need in order to manage IT properly, if we have a holistic and integrated set of solutions in IT. This is becoming all the more relevant as we are growing our ecosystem with more partners, and we need to be able to exchange information. We believe the only way we can actually achieve that, is by building out an open standard – and that is exactly what The Open Group delivers. I believe that this is going to make the difference in the IT industry, making it mature and much more professional and we all stand to benefit from that."
(Karel van Zeeland, Lead IT4IT Architect at Shell)

A.1.4 An IT4IT Governance Model

An essential component of an IT capability is to define and implement a governance model of how the IT function should be designed, operated, and supported. This section provides a brief overview of how the IT management capabilities are governed and managed within Shell. The vision of Shell is that IT management capabilities should be put under a single governance model with an IT executive owner. This helps to safeguard IT management capability improvements and investments.

Key entities involved in the IT4IT governance model at Shell are:
- Sponsorship at the IT executive leadership team (the CIO and IT executives)
- A center of excellence responsible for defining how the IT function should work (defining best practices and "one way of working") – this is internally within Shell referred to as the "Functional Excellence" team
- The IT4IT architecture team (with the lead IT4IT architect)
- The IT4IT delivery organization (headed by an IT4IT manager) responsible for the delivery and management of all IT management solutions within the IT4IT portfolio

The IT executive leadership team is the single governance and key decision-making body for the entire IT function. This team is collectively accountable for the overall strategic direction, performance, annual IT expenditure, and leadership of the IT function. This team is headed by the Group CIO of Shell.

Shell is convinced that IT management tools need to be managed as one integrated portfolio similar to other business IT portfolios. This enables Shell to optimize and rationalize the IT management applications used to support IT processes. Therefore, the accountability to develop and manage IT management solutions is assigned to one organization also called "IT4IT". This is similar to other global IT solutions such as within the HR, procurement, facility, and financial domains. The IT4IT delivery organization manages the standardized set of solutions to support the IT function such as application and project portfolio, Enterprise Architecture system, test management tools, ITSM system, CMDB, and monitoring tools. These IT management solutions are delivered as a service (IT4IT as a service) to all the different IT departments and user communities.

The IT4IT architect is part of the overall IT architecture community within the IT organization. The IT4IT architect governs the overall architecture of all IT management solutions as part of the IT4IT capability. The IT4IT architect uses the IT4IT Reference Architecture as the blueprint. This architect provides the end-to-end view of how processes, tools, and data should be designed and integrated. This person also engages with IT tool vendors and monitors market developments related to IT management.

Another team has been formed (a kind of center of excellence) which is responsible for working with practitioners across IT to facilitate best practices, standardize processes, and continuously improve them. This team is responsible for defining how the IT function is organized and supported by standard practices, processes, and common data models. The center of excellence is organized around a group of capabilities (and IT processes) similar to the IT4IT value streams. For each of these value streams there are sponsors defined at executive level to ensure there is sufficient support at the level of the CIO. The activities of the center of excellence are governed by the IT executive leadership team that reviews and approves proposed plans and investments and monitors progress.

Shell has been working for a considerable time to standardize and rationalize the portfolio of applications that are used to manage the IT function. With this IT4IT governance model, Shell has a unique proposition in having a dedicated IT4IT organization managing the portfolio, architecture, development, and operations of the IT management solutions. The IT4IT organization provides the standard toolkit to support capabilities such as application portfolio management, Project Portfolio Management (PPM) tool, Enterprise Architecture, test management, CMDB, IT financial management, and so on. Not many multi-nationals have this enterprise scale, standardized common processes and standard IT management tooling landscape that is available within Shell. For example, there is one single enterprise-wide ITSM system for managing incidents, problems, and changes; a standard request management portal for service requests from a service catalog; one global project management system, one federated CMDB, one Information Rights Management (IRM) system, and so on. Shell IT4IT has implemented a number of truly global enterprise solutions – including standard processes and guidelines – that are delivered as a service to all internal IT departments. Table 5 provides a number of examples of these global enterprise IT4IT solutions.

Table 5: Shell Examples of Global Enterprise IT4IT Solution

Value Stream	IT Management Solution	Description
Strategy to Portfolio	• Integrated service/application and Project Portfolio Management (PPM) • Enterprise Architecture (EA) system	• Manage portfolio of IT services and related projects (and investments in them) • Manage Enterprise Architecture
Requirement to Deploy	• Standard development and test management platform (referred to as SEDE) including source code management	• Include build and test automation
Request to Fulfill	• Standard self-service portal (my request)	• Self-service request portal; for example, to request a new laptop, access to business applications, or new infrastructure resources such as servers or databases
Detect to Correct	• ITSM system • Integrated monitoring and event management system (business service management) • Integrated security event management system	• Standard monitoring systems, ticketing system for managing all incidents, problems and changes integrated with the external service providers

Value Stream	IT Management Solution	Description
Supporting Activities	• IRM system • Federated CMDB (with discovery) • Software Asset Management (SAM) system • IT Business Management (ITBM) for financial transparency	• Standard information risk management system to manage risks, compliance, and findings • Integrated CMDB • Standard IT financial reporting per IT service or application (based upon actual consumption)

Integration between IT management tools becomes more and more important to enable the sharing of data. This requires a standard IT information model to enable data exchange and consolidation. An example in this area is the IT financial management reporting solution within Shell referred to as IT Business Management (ITBM). This solution collects data from many different IT administrations to understand the cost of an application or IT service. This requires a consistent data model to link projects to applications, configuration items to applications, contracts and licenses to applications, infrastructure costs to configuration items, and so on. An important foundation of the IT4IT solution is the central repository covering all IT services and applications. All activities within the IT organization are linked to this service portfolio such as linking projects to the application, linking costs, contracts and infrastructure components, or incidents and changes.

A.1.5 Learnings and Conclusion

This section highlights the key learnings from the IT4IT approach adopted at Shell:
- Set up a governance model to manage the IT management capabilities from a process, data, and tooling perspective (IT4IT delivery unit, IT4IT architect).
- Ensure IT executive sponsorship for IT management (at the level of the CIO).
- Provide architectural guidance for IT management capabilities by assigning an enterprise-wide IT4IT architect.
- Manage all IT management solutions as a single and integrated portfolio, defining clear ownership and accountability.
- Set up a central IT4IT organization to design, build, deploy, and operate IT management tools, providing IT management tools as a service (IT4IT as a service).

- Build a standardized and rationalized IT4IT tooling portfolio aligned with the IT management practices and changing IT management demands, and build strategic relationships with a limited number of IT management vendors.
- Build a community within the IT function to define standard practices and engage with IT specialists to continually capture feedback to improve the IT management capabilities.
- Ensure tool selections are governed by the IT4IT delivery organization, IT4IT architecture, and IT functional excellence team.
- Use The Open Group IT4IT Reference Architecture as a blueprint to analyze the current state; assess opportunities for improvement and agree on the target state.
- Define an IT4IT roadmap guiding future investments and supporting improvement opportunities.
- The roadmap of implementing IT4IT depends upon the maturity of the current IT management capabilities. Therefore, it is essential to analyze the current state and determine the most important next steps.

A.2   Rabobank

Rabobank[4] is an international, privately held bank based in the Netherlands. Originally founded by farmers as a cooperative bank for and by its customers, today Rabobank is one of the largest banks in the retail financial services market in the Netherlands. The bank also aims to be the best bank in the international food and agribusiness sectors. With significant global presence in more than 40 countries, the bank has more than 45,000 employees and 8.8 million customers worldwide with specialized services focused on programs such as asset management, real estate, and insurance.

Like many industries, the banking and financial services sector is under increasing pressure and competition due to digitalization. The pressure to deliver more services online, to do it faster, and to meet customer expectations for speed, efficiency, and excellent service has never been greater. At the same time, banks are also facing added pressure due to increased regulation, cyber attacks, and security issues. Rapid change – and the need to adapt to it quickly – is the new normal.

---

4   Rabobank™ is a trademark of Coöperatieve Centrale Raiffeisen-Boerenleenbank BA.

As a response to these challenges, Rabobank understood it needed to better manage its IT processes to meet the demands of customers, increased competition, and a changing business climate.

A.2.1 Background

According to Toine Jenniskens, a business architect responsible for managing all of the bank's IT processes and models:

"Rabobank has always been at the forefront of using automated IT management processes for aligning the company's IT and business goals. In fact, the bank was one of the first companies outside of the UK to adopt the ITIL standard in the mid-1980s."

In the early 2000s, Jenniskens became a manager in Rabobank's IT department and began advocating for the company's IT processes to be automated to facilitate better communications and break down silos throughout the organization. As the IT department began to automate its processes, they quickly learned that this was the way to go:

"We recognized early on that having an end-to-end value stream-based approach to IT would be very important and that IT needed to bridge the gap among different silos within the organization."

A.2.2 The Problem

As the IT department began automating its IT management activities, it looked into a variety of automated solutions from various IT vendors. With a growing portfolio of IT management solutions, Rabobank soon realized that a more sophisticated integration and interoperability is necessary to better serve the business. Meanwhile the business has become significantly more demanding on the IT function. Increased demand for developing new services, as well as a need for greater continuity of services in production and faster time to market, was placing additional pressure on Rabobank's IT development and operations departments.

Rabobank's IT culture also had to change to become more agile, while still meeting information security and compliance requirements as well as continuity demand in a reliable manner.

A.2.3 The Solution

To meet changing industry and customer requirements, Rabobank's IT department decided it needed to fully automate its entire IT delivery processes, from build to test and release through to deployment.

When Rabobank first embarked on this journey in 2007, the company "started off with a fantasy" that it might be able to find one vendor which could automate all of the IT processes. Although the simultaneous emergence of cloud computing models was making IT process automation easier, Rabobank soon realized that there is no all-encompassing IT automation and management solution on the market today. To enable effective and efficient IT service delivery, integration and standardization is needed across multiple IT management solutions.

Using both the TOGAF standard for defining Enterprise Architecture and an early release of The Open Group IT4IT Reference Architecture for managing the business of IT, Rabobank began to integrate its IT management solutions across the entire company with the following goals in mind:

- Create a clear and common understanding of Rabobank's loosely-coupled IT.
- Design one common service model for the API level (the service backbone).
- Implement an Agile-based culture across IT.
- Provide direct feedback (or showback) of usage and costs.
- Automate all of Rabobank's IT processes, including:
  - All manual tasks and processes (build, test, release, deploy, monitoring, and incident remediation)
  - Tooling
  - Identity and Access Management (IAM) (or rights management)

Because Rabobank had already standardized on ITIL, the company also wanted to take a standardized approach to further integrating its IT processes. With no overarching IT management solution available on the market, Rabobank realized it needed to consolidate management across multiple solutions. As such, they created both a consolidated monitoring platform and a consolidated service management platform, underpinned with a common data model. Without this consolidation, Rabobank would have to integrate 50 service management solutions. Instead, they could start automating their processes based on what they already had in place.

The IT organization got senior management involved to help determine their governance models, what to automate first, and also to help them present businesses cases that would necessitate automated workloads. IT teams, such as the .NET and Java teams, then developed further initiatives from there.

The TOGAF standard was used to help in Rabobank's approach to creating its IT management architecture. As such, the company moved from a rules-based to a principles-based architecture. In addition, the TOGAF framework helped the IT department discuss "why" the approach they chose to take was important for the business. The IT4IT framework, on the other hand, was used primarily to develop the department's strategy and models for how IT could be managed and automated.

A.2.4 The Result

Rabobank has taken a "manager of managers" approach in building out its current management platforms. Although the company would like to eventually use one solution, with no all-encompassing solution on the market today, they are currently taking a "community" solutions approach, using multiple solutions to manage their IT assets, grouped by individual vendor solutions. For example, they use SAP Solution Manager for the company's SAP landscape, Enterprise Manager for Oracle products, and Microsoft's SCOM, TFS etc. for their Microsoft environments. IT management tools from Hewlett Packard Enterprise are used at the macro level to manage and administer all of those solutions.

Rabobank has begun its long-term roadmap by automating its maintenance tasks and delivery of Linux and Windows servers with self-service. They are also in the process of automating much of their build and deployment capabilities for development.

Although the initiative is still underway, Rabobank is already seeing significant results. Automating their management solutions has significantly sped up timeframes for getting things done.

"Everything is just a faster process," Jenniskens says.

Implementing Agile and Lean processes has also allowed Rabobank to step up how they manage things.

"Now we really are developing our DevOps methodology in our IT management world," he says.

Rabobank's IT department and developers are able to move much faster because they now have a common understanding of how the company's IT management process works. The IT4IT framework is directly responsible for this result. In addition, the framework has helped them to better understand where there might be duplication within IT and decide which tools they need and which they don't.

Ultimately, the result thus far has been faster, more efficient business processes. Rather than having time lapses between projects, now the bank is able to practice continuous iteration, and IT is no longer a bottleneck for getting things done.

A.2.5 Looking Forward

In conjunction with the project, Rabobank's IT department recently revised it mission statement and purpose to refocus on three new areas:
- Know what to build
- Automate everything
- Monitor everything

To do that, the next step in the process is to rebuild a number of the department's applications to make them cloud-ready and to also enable automated delivery. In addition, IT intends to continue its focus on using Agile in order to keep processes on track.

The benefit of market standards such as the IT4IT or TOGAF standards is they are or will be proven and tested. In the financial services industry, using open-source solutions can be risky. A business like a bank can't be dependent on a solution that may not exist in a couple of years. That is why standardization is important for companies like Rabobank.

Jenniskens also says he hopes that groups such as The Open Group IT4IT Forum will further facilitate automation for IT management solutions across the industry:

"The next step would be to integrate between vendors in the IT community. We need integrated solutions across everything, but I think we're still very far from that."

IT4IT Reference Architecture and Other Best Practices

This appendix summarizes how the IT4IT Reference Architecture can be mapped to other relevant best practice frameworks and standards.

The IT4IT Reference Architecture provides the end-to-end IT operating model which describes how the entire IT function should be operated. In addition to the IT4IT standard, a number of other best practices and standards can be applied such as PMBOK, ITIL, and SCRUM. These best practices can provide additional guidance for specific functions or processes.

Not all the mentioned standards or practices are relevant or needed to build an all-embracing IT management model. This is due to the fact that there are significant overlaps between these practices and a number of them are not commonly applied (limited adoption in the market).

The recommended approach is as follows:
- Use the value streams as the overall framework to organize IT capabilities, data, and processes.
- Use the IT4IT Reference Architecture as the overall model to define the new IT operating model.
- Select a limited number of additional standards and best practices where relevant (such as PMBOK, ITIL, and SCRUM).

B.1 IT4IT Value Stream Mapping to Other Best Practices and Standards

Table 6 provides a mapping of the IT4IT value streams to related best practices, frameworks, and standards.

Table 6: Mapping IT4IT to Relevant IT Best Practices and Standards

Value Stream	Area	Example of Key Practices, Frameworks, and Standards
(Overall)	IT Service Management (ITSM) (full lifecycle)	<ul><li>ITIL</li><li>COBIT</li><li>ISO/IEC 20000 (IT Service Management)</li><li>ASL</li><li>BiSL</li><li>ISO/IEC 16350 (Application Management)</li><li>Information Technology Capability Maturity Framework (IT-CMF)</li></ul>
Strategy to Portfolio (S2P)	Enterprise Architecture	<ul><li>The TOGAF Standard</li><li>The ArchiMate Standard (for modeling)</li></ul>
	Project and Portfolio Management	<ul><li>PMBOK</li><li>PRINCE2</li><li>Managing Successful Programs (MSP)</li><li>ISO 21500 (Project Management)</li><li>Management of Portfolios (MoP)</li><li>Management of Value (MoV)</li><li>Portfolio, Program, and Project Offices (P3O) guidance</li></ul>
Requirement to Deploy (R2D)	Software Engineering	<ul><li>CMMI for Development</li><li>SCRUM</li><li>Scaled Agile Framework (SAFe)</li><li>Dynamic Systems Development Method (DSDM)</li><li>Rational Unified Process (RUP)</li><li>Software Engineering Body of Knowledge (SWEBOK)</li></ul>
	Test Management	<ul><li>ISO/IEC/IEEE 29119 (Software Testing)</li><li>ISO/IEC 25010 (Software Quality)</li></ul>
Detect to Correct (D2C)		<ul><li>ITIL</li><li>COBIT</li><li>CMMI for Services</li><li>ASL</li><li>ISM Method</li></ul>

Value Stream	Area	Example of Key Practices, Frameworks, and Standards
Supporting Activities	Security Management	• ISO/IEC 27000 series
	Continual Improvement Process (or also called Continuous Improvement)	• Lean IT • Six Sigma • Kaizen
	Sourcing	• CMMI for Acquisitions • Information Services Procurement Library (ISPL) • e-Sourcing Capability Model (e-SCM) • Outsourcing Professional Body of Knowledge (OPBOK)
	Software Asset Management	• ISO/IEC 19770 (Asset Management)
	Skills and Competence Management	• SFIA • European e-Competence (e-CF)
	Quality Management	• ISO 9000/ISO 9001 (Quality Management)
	IT Governance	• ISO/IEC 38500 (Governance)
	Risk Management	• Management of Risks (MoR) • ISO 31000 (Risk Management)

There are, however, many more IT management models, practices, and techniques – not mentioned in Table 6 – that provide additional guidance for specific IT activities such as methods for problem analytics, root cause analysis, risk analysis, Lean Kanban, Six Sigma, Test-Driven Development, UML for requirements and design, or various development and coding guidelines. For example, UML can be used as a technique to capture user stories and application designs.

B.2   ITIL and COBIT Mapping

The following diagrams show how ITIL processes, as the primary process model used within the IT industry, can be mapped upon the IT4IT Reference Architecture.

Figure 36 shows a high-level positioning of value streams on the ITIL service lifecycle model.

Mapping IT4IT Value Streams to ITIL

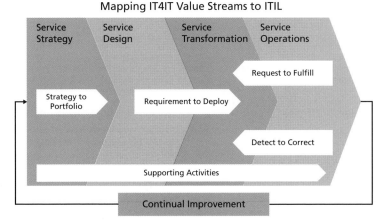

Figure 36: IT4IT Value Streams Positioned Against ITIL Service Lifecycle Phases

Figure 37 shows the mapping of ITIL processes to the IT4IT value streams. This diagram only shows processes as described by ITIL V3. ITIL, however, has a number of process gaps such as Enterprise Architecture, Project Management and Service Development.

Strategy to Portfolio	Requirement to Deploy	Request to Fulfill	Detect to Correct
ITIL Process Mapping			
Business Relationship Management	Transition Planning and Support	Service Catalog Management	Event Management
Strategy Management for IT Services	Design Coordination	Request Fulfilment	Incident Management
	Service Validation & Testing	Access Management	
Demand Management			Problem Management
	Release & Deployment Management		
Service Portfolio Management	Change Management & Change Evaluation		
Supporting Activities			
Financial Management for IT Services			
Service Asset & Configuration Management			
Knowledge Management			
Availability Management			
Service Level Management			
Supplier Management			
Information Security Management			
IT Service Continuity Management			
Capacity Management			
The Seven-step Improvement Process			

Figure 37: Mapping ITIL to the IT Value Chain

Table 7 provides a short overview of the differences between ITIL and the IT4IT Reference Architecture.

Table 7: Differences between ITIL and the IT4IT Reference Architecture

Attribute	ITIL	IT4IT Reference Architecture
Characteristics	Framework describing functions/capabilities/ disciplines.	Information model-driven reference architecture, supportive of multiple process frameworks.
Origins	An aggregate of best practices drawn from a world-wide community of executives, managers, and individual contributors.	Driven by specific needs of Enterprise Architects and IT managers.
Form	Primarily narrative.	Primarily architectural, framed using the TOGAF standard and presented using the ArchiMate language.
Utility	Oriented to education.	Solution-orientation; usable "off-the-shelf".
Value Proposition	Enable detailed analysis at the function process level.	Enables choreography of four high-level value streams (Strategy to Portfolio, Requirement to Deploy, Request to Fulfill, Detect to Correct) and offers prescriptive guidance for the design of products and services that deliver them.
Structure		Mutually-exclusive and comprehensive architectural catalogs.
Granularity		Precise and prescriptive representation of data and integration patterns for the whole IT management domain.
Agility	Implicit waterfall, top-down planning orientation.	Explicit accommodation of Agile and DevOps trends and Lean Kanban approaches.
Provenance	Evolved through various proprietary ownerships.	Dynamic, open peer-to-peer development and review processes under the aegis of The Open Group.

Table 8 provides a more detailed list of related practices grouped per value stream.

Table 8: Detailed List of Related Practices Grouped per Value Stream

IT4IT Value Stream	IT4IT Reference Architecture Functional Component	ITIL V3	COBIT 5	Other Guidelines, Frameworks, and Best Practices
Strategy to Portfolio (S2P)	Enterprise Architecture	• Strategy Management for IT Services	• APO01 Manage the IT Management Framework	• Enterprise Architecture (the TOGAF Standard)
	Policy	• Service Portfolio Management	• APO02 Manage Strategy	• Project Management (PMBOK/PMI)
	Proposal	• Demand Management	• APO03 Manage Enterprise Architecture	• Management of Portfolios (MoP)
	Portfolio Demand	• Business Relationship Management (BRM)	• APO04 Manage Innovation	• Managing Successful Programs (MSP)
	Service Portfolio	• Capacity Management	• APO05 Manage Portfolio	• Management of Value (MoV)
			• APO08 Manage Relationships	• Portfolio, Program, and Project Offices (P3O) guidance
			• BAI01 Manage Programs and Projects	• BRM Body of Knowledge (BOK)
			• BAI04 Manage Availability and Capacity	• Val IT Framework
				• ASL
				• BiSL
Requirement to Deploy (R2D)	Project	• Transition Planning & Support	• BAI01 Manage Programs and Projects	• Project Management (PRINCE2)
	Requirement	• Design Coordination	• BAI02 Manage Requirements Definition	• Project Management (PMBOK/PMI)
	Service Design	• Change Management	• BAI03 Manage Solution Identification and Build	• CMMI for Development
	Source Control	• Service Validation & Testing	• BAI05 Manage Organizational Change Enablement	• Scaled Agile Framework (SAFe)
	Build	• Release & Deployment Management	• BAI06 Manage Changes	• SCRUM
	Build Package	• Change Evaluation	• BAI07 Manage Change Acceptance and Transitioning	• ASL
	Release Composition			• BiSL
	Test			• Dynamic Systems Development Method (DSDM)
	Defect			• Rational Unified Process (RUP)
				• Software Engineering Body of Knowledge (SWEBOK)
				• Business Analysis Body of Knowledge (BABOK) guidance

IT4IT Value Stream	IT4IT Reference Architecture Functional Component	ITIL V3	COBIT 5	Other Guidelines, Frameworks, and Best Practices
Request to Fulfill (R2F)	Engagement Experience Portal	• Service Catalog Management	• APO09 Manage Service Agreements	
	Offer Consumption	• Service Level Management	• DSS02 Manage Service Requests and Incidents	
	Offer Management	• Request Fulfillment	• BAI04 Manage Availability and Capacity	
	Catalog Composition	• Access Management	• BAI06 Manage Changes	
	Request Rationalization	• Release & Deployment Management	• BAI08 Management Knowledge	
	Fulfillment Execution	• Capacity Management		
	Usage	• Change Management		
	Chargeback/ Showback	• Change Evaluation		
	Knowledge & Collaboration			
Detect to Correct (D2C)	Service Monitoring	• Event Management	• DSS01 Manage Operations	• CMMI for Services
	Event	• Incident Management	• DSS02 Manage Service Requests and Incidents	• ASL
	Incident	• Problem Management	• DSS03 Manage Problems	• BiSL
	Problem	• Information Security Management (ISMS)	• DSS04 Manage Continuity	• ISM Method
	Change Control	• IT Service Continuity Management	• APO09 Manage Service Agreements	
	Configuration Management	• Service Asset & Configuration Management	• APO13 Manage Security	
	Diagnostics and Remediation	• Service Level Management	• BAI04 Manage Availability and Capacity	
	Service Level	• Availability Management	• BAI06 Manage Changes	
		• Capacity Management		
		• Change Management		

IT4IT Value Stream	IT4IT Reference Architecture Functional Component	ITIL V3	COBIT 5	Other Guidelines, Frameworks, and Best Practices
Supporting Activities	Governance, Risk and, Compliance (GRC)	• Information Security Management (ISMS) • IT Service Continuity Management	• EDM01 Ensure Governance Framework Setting and Maintenance • EDM02 Ensure Benefits Delivery • EDM03 Ensure Risk Optimization • EDM04 Ensure Resource Optimization • EDM05 Ensure Stakeholder Transparency • APO12 Manage Risk • APO13 Manage Security • DSS04 Manage Continuity • DSS05 Manage Security Services • DSS06 Manage Business Process Controls • MEA02 Monitor, Evaluate, and Assess the Systems of Internal Control • MEA03 Monitor and Evaluate Compliance with External Requirements	• ISO/IEC 38500 (Governance) • ISO/IEC 27000 series • Management of Risks (MoR) • ISO 31000 (Risk Management)
	Sourcing & Vendor	• Supplier Management • Service Level Management	• APO09 Service Level Management • APO10 Manage Suppliers	• Service Integration and Management (SIAM) • CMMI for Acquisitions • Information Services Procurement Library (ISPL) • e-Sourcing Capability Model (e-SCM) • Outsourcing Professional Body of Knowledge (OPBOK)

IT4IT Value Stream	IT4IT Reference Architecture Functional Component	ITIL V3	COBIT 5	Other Guidelines, Frameworks, and Best Practices
	Intelligence & Reporting	• Knowledge Management • The Seven-step Improvement Process	• MEA1 Monitor and Evaluate Performance and Conformance • APO11 Manage Quality	• Balanced Scorecard
	Finance & Assets	• Financial Management for IT Services • Service Asset & Configuration Management	• APO06 Manage Budget and Cost • BAI09 Manage Assets • BIA10 Manage Configuration	• Technology Business Management (TBM)
	Resource & Project	• Capacity Management • Availability Management	• APO07 Manage Human Resources • BAI01 Manage Programs and Projects • BAI04 Manage Availability and Capacity	• SFIA • European e-Competence (e-CF) • Project Management (PRINCE2) • Project Management (PMBOK/PMI)

Appendix C

IT4IT Tool Categories

A key aspect of the IT4IT approach is the automation of IT management activities through the value stream. The following table provides an overview of different types of applications supporting the functional components in the IT4IT Reference Architecture. This can be used a checklist for the "as-is" analysis as well as for discussing capabilities with software vendors.

IT4IT Value Stream	IT4IT Reference Architecture Functional Component	IT4IT Tool Categories/IT4IT Tool Repositories (Examples)
Strategy to Portfolio (S2P)	Enterprise Architecture	• Enterprise architecture system including business process modeling • Data modeling tools • Architecture auditing tools • Business process modeling tools
	Policy	• EA system • Policy management system
	Proposal	• Project Portfolio Management (PPM) • ITSM system
	Portfolio Demand	• Project Portfolio Management (PPM) • Enterprise Portfolio Management (EPM) • IT Business Management (ITBM) tools • Agile development tools (for managing the portfolio backlog)
	Service Portfolio	• EA system • Application Portfolio Management (APM) • Enterprise Portfolio Management (EPM) • Roadmap systems • Service improvement register • Customer (satisfaction) survey tools

IT4IT Value Stream	IT4IT Reference Architecture Functional Component	IT4IT Tool Categories/IT4IT Tool Repositories (Examples)
Requirement to Deploy (R2D)	Project	• Project Portfolio Management (PPM) tool (to manage project tasks, risks, plans, etc.) • Agile development tools for tracking all activities and related plans such as release and sprint plans
	Requirement	• Requirements management system (part of an ALM system); e.g., to manage requirements, themes, epics, user stories • See also design tools (e.g., mockup and story-boarding tools)
	Service Design	• Design and prototyping tools (mockup, wireframe and user interface prototyping tools) • Story-boarding tools • Document management tools (and content management) • UML design tool • EA tools • SOA register • …
	Source Control	• Integrated Development Environment (IDE) • Code editors, debuggers, and compilers • Source control repositories (SCM) system
	Build	• Build and Continuous Integration (CI) tools • Artifact repositories
	Build Package	
	Release Composition	• Artifact repositories • Packaging tools • Release and deployment management tool • Definitive Media Library (DML)

IT4IT Value Stream	IT4IT Reference Architecture Functional Component	IT4IT Tool Categories/IT4IT Tool Repositories (Examples)
	Test	• Unit testing tools • Test management system • Performance, load, and/or stress management tool • Test data management • Test automation tools • Security testing tools • Code quality checks • Static code analysis • Service virtualization • ...
	Defect	• Defect management system (often part of a test management tool)
Request to Fulfill (R2F)	Engagement Experience Portal	• Request management system • IT Service Management (ITSM) system • Self-service portal (web shop) • Content Management System (CMS) • Knowledge base • Collaboration and communication tools
	Offer Consumption	• Request management system • Self-service portal (web shop) • Customer survey tool
	Offer Management	• Request management system
	Catalog Composition	• Request management system • Service catalog management tool
	Request Rationalization	• Request management system • Orchestration tools • CMDB (or subscription administrations) • Identity and Access Management (IAM) tools

IT4IT Value Stream	IT4IT Reference Architecture Functional Component	IT4IT Tool Categories/IT4IT Tool Repositories (Examples)
	Fulfillment Execution	• Release and deployment management tool • Provisioning tools • Run book automation tool • Orchestration tools • Element managers (technology-specific management tools for desktops/laptops, network, storage, databases, operating systems, etc.) • Workload management tools • Identity and Access Management (IAM) tools • IT Service Management (ITSM) systems (standard change/standard request) • Cloud management tools (from cloud management vendors) • Cloud Management Platforms (CMP)
	Usage	• Monitoring tools for consumption and usage • Software metering • Identity and Access Management (IAM) tools
	Chargeback/Showback	• IT Financial Management (ITFM) tools • IT Business Management (ITBM) tools • Showback/chargeback tools • Reporting tools

Detect to Correct (D2C)	Service Monitoring	• Monitoring tools such as:
		  –Business Process Monitoring (BPM)
		  –Synthetic transactions or real-user monitoring
		  –Application Performance Monitoring (APM)
		  –Infrastructure monitoring such as hardware, software, operating systems, storage, network, etc.

IT4IT Value Stream	IT4IT Reference Architecture Functional Component	IT4IT Tool Categories/IT4IT Tool Repositories (Examples)
		−Security monitoring such as vulnerability scanning, intrusion detection, etc. (including DoS) −Log monitoring −Usage monitoring −Status monitoring −SLA monitoring • Element managers such as network, database, storage, and system management tools
	Event	• Event management system (including event correlation) • CMDB systems (for service impact)
	Incident	• Self-service portal (including self-help and self-ticketing) • Incident management tool (part of the ITSM system) • Customer survey tool • CMDB systems (for impact and investigation)
	Problem	• Problem management tool (part of the ITSM system) • Predictive analytic tools (including big data solutions) • Operations log analytics • CMDB systems (for impact and investigation)
	Change Control	• IT Service Management (ITSM) system • Change management tool (normal/emergency/standard change)
	Configuration Management	• Discovery/automated inventory (and configuration auditing tools) • Configuration Management System (CMS) • Configuration Management Database (CMDB) • Desktop management tools

IT4IT Value Stream	IT4IT Reference Architecture Functional Component	IT4IT Tool Categories/IT4IT Tool Repositories (Examples)
		• Element managers such as network, database, storage, and system management tools
	Diagnostics & Remediation	• Diagnostics tools • Orchestration tools in use for run book automation
	Service Level	• IT Service Management (ITSM) system (covering an incident management tool) • CMDB or contract management system • Service monitoring tool • Reporting system/Business Intelligence (BI)
Supporting Activities	Governance, Risk, and Compliance (GRC)	• IT GRC tool • Risk assessment tools • IT risk management system • IT control register • Security Management Information System (SMIS)
	Sourcing and Vendor	• Procurement and contract management system
	Intelligence and Reporting	• Business Intelligence (BI) tools such as IT data warehouse, reporting tools, dashboards, scorecards • Operations analytics tools • Document management system • Knowledge base • Predictive business analytic tools (including big data solutions)
	Finance and Assets	• IT Financial Management (ITFM) system • General ledger and accounts payable • Fixed asset register • Investment Portfolio Management (IPM)

IT4IT Value Stream	IT4IT Reference Architecture Functional Component	IT4IT Tool Categories/IT4IT Tool Repositories (Examples)
		• Budget management and planning tools • Configuration Management System (CMS) • Configuration Management Database (CMDB) • Software Asset Management (SAM) system
	Resource and Project	• HR tools • HR resource planning tools • Training and education tools (e.g., learning systems) • Project management tools • Project planning tools • Time writing systems
Other	Technologies/Tools used both by Business and IT (shared)	• Document management tools • Financial management system • Procurement and contract management system • Time writing system • Communication and collaboration tools • Notification systems • Business Intelligence (BI)/reporting tools • Data warehouse • HR system

An IT organization needs to identify opportunities to automate IT management tasks. The following table provides an overview of IT automation tool options.

IT4IT Value Stream	IT4IT Reference Architecture Functional Component	IT4IT Tool Categories/IT4IT Tool Repositories (Examples)
Requirement to Deploy (R2D)	Build and Continuous Integration (CI)	Tools integrated with the overall application development platform to automatically build and integrate software from source code and artifact repositories.
	Test Automation	Running automated test scenarios triggered upon new builds and releases. This includes capabilities such as: • Unit testing • Functional testing • Service virtualization • Test data management • Stress and load testing • Security testing
Request to Fulfill (R2F)	Self-Service Request Portal	Portal to request services and modify subscriptions.
	Automated Provisioning and Deployment of Software and Access Rights	Automated provisioning through self-service portals using a standard service catalog. Terms used: • Deployment • Orchestration and run book automation • Infrastructure provisioning • Application release automation This includes IAM, software deployment, password resets, etc.
Detect to Correct (D2C)	Self-Service and Self-Help Portal	Use self-service portal for users and consumers to resolve incidents themselves using a knowledge base, diagnostic tools, etc.
	Service Monitoring	Automatically monitor and collect data about the availability, performance, and security aspects of IT services and infrastructure components. This includes, for example, robotic/synthetic transactions to simulate end-users.

IT4IT Value Stream	IT4IT Reference Architecture Functional Component	IT4IT Tool Categories/IT4IT Tool Repositories (Examples)
	Security and Risk Monitoring	A specific sub-category of service monitoring covers security, compliance, and risk monitoring such as: • Vulnerability scanning • Intrusion detection • Log monitoring
	Automated Discovery/ Inventory	Automatically collect configuration data, configuration changes, etc. Audit configuration settings.
	Orchestration and Run Book Automation	Orchestrate and automate IT tasks.
	Automated Recovery	Initiated automated response and recovery actions.
	Workload and Capacity Tuning	Ensure automated allocated of IT resources when needed based upon predefined policies (for example, add additional CPU or other resources in peak hours). Other examples: • Automatically scale resources • Turn resources on/off
	Software Metering and Usage Monitoring	Monitor actual usage of resources and applications.
	Predictive Analytics	Use analytics and machine learning capabilities.

IT4IT Data Entities

IT4IT Value Stream	IT4IT Reference Architecture Functional Component	Core Artifacts	Other Data Entities (Examples)
Strategy to Portfolio (S2P)	Enterprise Architecture	Service Architecture	• Business service • Business process • Business capability • Application architecture • IT standards • Data model • IT capability • Technology end-of-life data
	Policy	Policy	
	Proposal	Scope Agreement	• Proposal • Investment opportunity • Business case
	Portfolio Demand	Portfolio Backlog Item	• Theme • Epic • Demand • Idea
	Service Portfolio	• Conceptual Service • Conceptual Service Blueprint	• IT service portfolio • Application portfolio • Technology portfolio • IT roadmap • Service budget • Service performance • Service improvement opportunities (and improvement plan)

IT4IT Value Stream	IT4IT Reference Architecture Functional Component	Core Artifacts	Other Data Entities (Examples)
Requirement to Deploy (R2D)	Project	IT Initiative	• Project • Project cost • Project risks • Project plan • Project change request
	Requirement	Requirement	• Theme • Epic • Feature • User story
	Service Design	Logical Service Blueprint	• Design specifications • UML diagram • Use-case
	Source Control	Source	
	Build	Build	
	Build Package	Build Package	• Software package
	Release Composition	• Service Release • Service Release Blueprint	• Release package • Patches
	Test	Test Case	• Test plan • Test data
	Defect	Defect	
Request to Fulfill (R2F)	Engagement Experience Portal	User Profile	• Service catalog • Knowledge records
	Offer Consumption	Shopping Cart	
	Offer Management	• Offer • Offer Catalog	
	Catalog Composition	Service Catalog Entry	
	Request Rationalization	• Request • Subscription	• Access rights
	Fulfillment Execution	• Fulfillment Request • Desired Service Model	• Run book • Deployment packages • Service blueprint • Application topology

IT4IT Value Stream	IT4IT Reference Architecture Functional Component	Core Artifacts	Other Data Entities (Examples)
	Usage	Usage Record	• Consumption and usage data • Utilization data
	Chargeback/ Showback	Chargeback Contract	• IT costs
	Knowledge & Collaboration	• Knowledge • Conversation	
Detect to Correct (D2C)	Service Monitoring	Service Monitor	• Availability data • Performance data • Logs
	Event	Event	• Alarm • Security event (or vulnerabilities)
	Incident	• Incident • Interaction	• Incident SLA data • Vendor performance • Security incident
	Problem	• Problem • Known Error	
	Change Control	RFC	• Change schedule • Change approvals
	Configuration Management	Actual Service CI	• Configuration item • CI type • CI relationship (or interfaces) • Hardware assets • Models • End-of-life/end-of-support • Installed software • Contracts • Software licenses • Locations
	Diagnostics & Remediation	Run Book	

IT4IT Value Stream	IT4IT Reference Architecture Functional Component	Core Artifacts	Other Data Entities (Examples)
	Service Level	• Service Contract • KPI	• SLA, OLA, underpinning contracts
Supporting Activities	Governance, Risk, and Compliance (GRC)	• IT risk • IT control • IT audit	• Findings • Audit reports • Business Impact Assessment (BIA) • Security risks • Security policies
	Sourcing and Vendor	• Vendor • Contract	• Vendor performance
	Intelligence and Reporting	• KPI/metrics • Service reports	
	Finance and Assets	• IT budget • Actual cost • IT cost model • Invoice • Project costs	• Fixed asset • Cost center • Work breakdown structure • Cost categories • …
	Resource and Project	HR resource	• Training plans • Skill • Job profile • Support groups/teams • User identities • Roles and responsibilities • Organization structure

Glossary of Key Terms and Acronyms

ADM	Architecture Development Method
ALM	Application Lifecycle Management
API	Application Program Interface
APM	Application Performance Monitoring
APM	Application Portfolio Management
ARA	Application Release Automation
ASL	Application Services Library
BABOK	Business Analysis Body of Knowledge
BI	Business Intelligence
BIA	Business Impact Assessment
BiSL	Business Information Services Library
BRM	Business Relationship Management
BYOD	Bring Your Own Device
BYOT	Bring Your Own Tool
CI	Configuration Item
CI	Continuous Integration
CIO	Chief Information Officer
CMDB	Configuration Management Database
CMMI	Capability Maturity Model Integration
CMO	Current Mode of Operation
CMP	Cloud Management Platform
CMS	Configuration Management System
CMS	Content Management System
COBIT	Control Objectives for Information and Related Technology
CRA	Change Readiness Assessment
DML	Definitive Media Library
DoS	Denial of Service
DSDM	Dynamic Systems Development Method
EA	Enterprise Architecture
e-CF	European e-Competence Framework
EPM	Enterprise Portfolio Management
ERP	Enterprise Resource Planning

e-SCM	e-Sourcing Capability Model
FMO	Future Mode of Operation
FTE	Full-Time Equivalent
GRC	Governance, Risk, and Compliance
IaaS	Infrastructure as a Service
IAM	Identity and Access Management
IDE	Integrated Development Environment
IoT	Internet of Things
IP	Internet Procotol
IPM	Investment Portfolio Management
IRM	Information Rights Management
ISM	Integrated Service Management
ISMS	Information Security Management
ISPL	Information Services Procurement Library
IT	Information Technology
ITBM	IT Business Management
IT-CMF	Information Technology Capability Maturity Framework
ITIL	Information Technology Infrastructure Library
ITFM	IT Financial Management
ITSM	IT Service Management
KPI	Key Performance Indicator
MBWA	Management By Walking Around
MDM	Mobile Device Management
MoP	Management of Portfolios
MoR	Management of Risks
MoV	Management of Value
MSP	Managing Successful Programs
OLA	Operational-Level Agreement
OPBOK	Outsourcing Professional Body of Knowledge
P3O	Portfolio, Program, and Project Offices
PaaS	Platform as a Service
PLM	Product Lifecycle Management
PMBOK	Project Management Body of Knowledge
PMI	Project Management Institute
PMO	Project Management Office
PPM	Project Portfolio Management
REST	REpresentational State Transfer
RFC	Request for Change

RUP	Rational Unified Process
SaaS	Software as a Service
SAFe	Scaled Agile Framework
SAM	Software Asset Management
SAML	Security Assertion Markup Language
SCM	Supply Chain Management
SCOM	System Center Operations Manager
SDN	Software-Defined Networking
SFIA	Skills Framework for the Information Age
SIAM	Service Integration and Management
SLA	Service-Level Agreement
SMIS	Security Management Information System
SOA	Service-Oriented Architecture
SWEBOK	Software Engineering Body of Knowledge
TBM	Technology Business Management
TDD	Test-Driven Development
TFS	Team Foundation Server
UAT	User Acceptance Testing
UML	Unified Modeling Language
VLAN	Virtual Local Area Network
WBSE	Workplace for Business Strategy Execution

Index